BUSINESS SECRETS FROM THE BIBLE, WORKBOOK

BUSINESS SECRETS FROM THE BIBLE, WORKBOOK

Spiritual Success Strategies for Financial Abundance

SECOND EDITION

RABBI DANIEL LAPIN
AND SUSAN LAPIN

WILEY

Published by John Wiley & Sons, Inc., Hoboken, New Jersey.
Published simultaneously in Canada.

Library of Congress Cataloging-in-Publication Data Is Available:

ISBN 9781394215911 (Paperback)
ISBN 9781394215935 (ePDF)
ISBN 9781394215928 (ePub)

Cover Design: Wiley
Cover Image: © Polyanska Lyubov/Shutterstock

SKY10070820_032724

Contents

Introduction

You have begun reading *Business Secrets from the Bible: Spiritual Success Strategies for Financial Abundance*. Well done! That is part one of the program you embarked upon when you picked up your copy. Here is part two. And it is just as indispensable as part one.

We intuitively tend to think of information linearly, in the way perhaps that craftsmen would assemble cars before Ford's innovative assembly line in about 1910. A group of mechanics would work together building a car from the ground up. When it was done, they would move on to building the second car of the day. By the end of the day, they would have assembled six cars. If we stopped them at noon, we'd have three completed cars. It is a linear process.

Then came the first version of an early assembly line, and now the same component is added to 20 cars at a time. Then the headlights are installed on all 20 cars at a time. Then finally, by the end of the day, instead of only six finished cars, there would be 20. A more efficient way to build cars. However, if we stopped the process at noon, we would not have 10 cars; we'd have none.

Think of buying 10 apples at the market. If you're interrupted while putting apples in your basket, you'll still go home with, say, five apples. The remaining five are dispensable. You can still enjoy the five you bought. Contrast this with purchasing one of those gift cards at the same market. There are two steps to this purchase. Pick out the gift card you want from the gift card stand. That is step one. Now take it to a cashier who will activate the card for you by running it through a magnetic read/write device. If you're interrupted halfway and get the card but don't get it activated, you have nothing. Both steps are indispensable.

This is why we wrote above that this workbook is just as indispensable as the book it accompanies. The book provides the information. This workbook was designed to help you usefully deploy this information in your life.

Imagine we interviewed Usain Bolt just after he won the 100-meter race at the London Olympics in 2012 in just over nine and a half seconds.

"Can you tell us, Mr. Bolt," we'd ask, "what is the secret to running 100 meters in under 10 seconds?"

"Sure," he'd warmly respond. "It's easy. Just move your legs really fast."

And he's right. That is the secret. But to get to be able to move one's legs really fast, there are a great many steps. They have to do with training regimens, self-discipline, nutrition, and other necessary ingredients we can't even imagine.

The information in *Business Secrets from the Bible: Spiritual Success Strategies for Financial Abundance* is crucial. But now, making the information part of your being and incorporating it into your day-to-day life is equally crucial.

Throughout this workbook, you will find many exercises crafted to reinforce the key concepts from each chapter. They are also designed to encourage self-reflection, introspection, and actionable steps toward personal growth and financial empowerment. These include steps include the following:

1. Reflection Questions: These questions are meant to encourage you to think deeply about the concepts presented and how they relate to your own life. By answering these questions honestly, you will gain valuable insights into your beliefs, attitudes, and behaviors surrounding money and success. No one will mark your answers. The more truthful you can be with yourself, the more you will benefit.
2. Actionable Steps: The workbook is not just about theory; it is about practical application. We present actionable steps that challenge you to put the teachings into practice. These steps will help you implement the principles discussed and integrate them into your daily life.

3. Thought Exercises: Throughout the workbook, you will encounter thought exercises that explore varied scenarios and challenges related to the chapter's topic. These exercises encourage you to think critically, problem-solve, and develop a deeper understanding of the principles at play in real-life situations.
4. Guided Reflections: The workbook provides guided reflections to help you internalize each chapter's themes. These reflections enable you to connect with the concepts on a deeper level and make them a part of your mindset and decision-making process.

By actively engaging with the exercises in this workbook, you will embark on a powerful journey of self-discovery and growth. You will uncover the secrets to spiritual and financial success, transforming your perception of money, wealth, and service to others. Whether you are a seasoned business professional or just beginning your financial journey, these exercises will help equip you with the tools and mindset needed to thrive in both the material and spiritual realms.

So often, we buy a book, shake our heads approvingly at some of the ideas it contains, and forget those ideas by the next day. *Business Secrets from the Bible* is meant to be lived, more than read. If you review the workbook three months, six months, or more after your initial introduction to it, we hope that your answers to various exercises will reflect your growth.

Remember, the wisdom in *Business Secrets from the Bible* goes beyond business strategies; it delves into the very essence of our existence. Let us embark on this transformative journey together, exploring the secrets hidden within ancient scriptures and unlocking the path to financial success. Let's begin!

Secret #1

God Wants Each of Us to Be Obsessively Preoccupied with the Needs and Desires of His Other Children

Welcome to the fascinating world of *Business Secrets from the Bible, Workbook!* In this chapter, we begin a journey that uncovers the importance of interdependence, service, and specialization in the business world. Get ready to explore timeless principles that will transform your perspective on how to thrive in business while fostering meaningful connections with others.

These secrets will revolutionize the way you approach business, forge meaningful connections, and create a lasting impact. By embracing interdependence and specialization, you will set yourself on a path to thrive both in the business world and in the realm of human connection.

Let's embark on this enlightening journey and uncover the business secrets that lie within the enduring wisdom of the Bible.

Exercise 1.1

1. A______________ can be defined as any person or group that has customers.

2. ______________ refers to focusing on a specific area of expertise or skill.

3. Biblical examples, such as Jacob's blessings to his sons and ______________ blessings to the tribes, highlight the concept of unity with diversity.

4. The solitary survivalist tends to view others as a(n) ______________.

5. ______________ wrote about being alone, that, ".... the life of man [is] solitary, poor, nasty, brutish, and short."

Answers:

1. Business; 2. Specialization; 3. Moses'; 4. threat; 5. Thomas Hobbes

Exercise 1.2 Self-assessment: Discover Your Strengths

Having explored the importance of interdependence, service, and specialization in the business world, it's time to turn our focus inward. Take a moment to reflect on your own strengths, passions, and skills. By understanding your unique qualities, you will identify areas where you can specialize and excel. This self-assessment will help you gain insights into your potential areas of specialization.

Self-assessment Questionnaire

1. What skills or talents come naturally to you?
2. What activities or tasks do you enjoy the most? What energizes you?
3. Do you find yourself drawn to specific subjects or areas of knowledge?
4. What feedback have you received from others about your strengths or stand-out qualities?
5. When faced with challenges, which skills or approaches do you tend to rely on?
6. Are there activities or tasks where you consistently outperform others?
7. What are your proudest accomplishments? What skills did you utilize to achieve them?
8. When working in a team or group, which roles or responsibilities do you naturally gravitate toward?
9. What activities or tasks do you find fulfilling, even if they require effort or dedication?
10. If you had unlimited time and resources, what skills or knowledge would you love to acquire or develop further?

Exercise 1.3 Identify Your Areas of Specialization

Consider your responses and look for patterns, recurring themes, or standout strengths that emerge. Be honest with yourself and tune into your instincts.

Next, create a list of potential areas of specialization based on your reflections. These can be specific skills, subject matters, or even industries where you believe you can excel. Write them down, allowing yourself to explore various possibilities.

Once you have your list, review each potential specialization, and ask yourself the following questions:

- Which areas align with my passions and interests?
- Where do I see opportunities for growth and development?
- How can I apply my unique strengths and skills to make a positive impact in these areas?
- Which specializations excite and inspire me the most?

By narrowing down your list and identifying areas where you can specialize, you are setting the foundation for a fulfilling and successful journey. Remember, specialization allows you to channel your energy, time, and resources into areas where you can truly excel and make a meaningful difference.

Take the time to reflect on your self-assessment and revisit it periodically. As you grow and evolve, your areas of specialization may shift or expand. Be open to new possibilities and opportunities that come your way.

Exercise 1.4 Guided Reflection and Action Plan

Take a moment to engage in this guided reflection exercise and create an action plan that will guide your future actions. Follow the prompts below:

Reflection

- Think about your current business or professional life. How do you currently approach interdependence, serving others, and specialization?
- Reflect on the benefits and rewards highlighted in the chapter. How do you envision these principles enhancing your own success, fulfillment, and impact?

Welcoming Interdependence

- Identify areas where you can collaborate and foster mutually beneficial relationships with others in your industry or community.
- Determine how you can leverage the strengths and expertise of others to enhance your own work or projects.
- Write down specific actions you will take to actively seek out opportunities for collaboration and interdependence.

Specialization

- Review the list of your unique strengths, passions, and areas of expertise from Exercise 1.3.
- Reflect on how you can narrow your focus and specialize in a specific aspect of your field.
- Research whether this is a marketable specialty.
- Consider the benefits of specialization, such as increased efficiency, improved quality, and the ability to deliver exceptional value.
- Write down specific actions you will take to further develop and specialize in your chosen field.

Integration and Accountability

- Create a timeline or schedule for implementing these actions, setting specific milestones and deadlines.
- Consider sharing your action plan with a trusted colleague, mentor, or accountability partner who can provide support and hold you accountable.

Remember!

Applying these principles is a journey, and it may take time and effort to fully embrace interdependence and specialization. Be patient with yourself and allow room for growth and learning along the way.

By completing this reflection exercise and creating your action plan, you are taking the first steps toward integrating these valuable lessons into your own life and business.

Keep this action plan somewhere visible as a reminder of your commitment, and regularly revisit it to assess your progress and make necessary adjustments. With each step, you will move closer to realizing your full potential and achieving both personal and professional success.

Best of luck on your journey of interdependence and specializing in your chosen field!

Summary and Encouragement

Throughout this chapter, we have explored the key lessons of interdependence and finding fulfillment through specialization. These principles hold immense significance in both our personal and professional lives. Let's recap the key takeaways and reiterate their importance:

1. Interdependence: We are not meant to navigate life or business alone. Interdependence allows us to tap into the collective strengths and resources of others. By fostering collaborative relationships and relying on one another's expertise, we can achieve greater success and overcome challenges more effectively.
2. Specialization: By focusing on our unique strengths, passions, and skills, we can specialize in a specific area. Specialization allows us to deliver exceptional value, increase efficiency, and stand out in a crowded marketplace. It empowers us to become experts in our chosen fields and opens doors to new opportunities for growth and success.

Interdependence and specializing intertwine and reinforce one another. By incorporating these principles into your life and business, you can create a positive ripple effect, fostering meaningful relationships and achieving both personal and professional fulfillment.

Take these lessons to heart and let them guide your actions. By doing so, you will not only thrive in your endeavors but also contribute to a more interconnected and prosperous world.

Wishing you great success and fulfillment on this journey!

Secret #2

An Infinite God Created Us in His Image with Infinite Imagination, Potential, Creative Power, and Desires

Imagine a world where everyone stops working and where ambition fades away. Picture the impact on your daily life and the functioning of society. We rely on each other's ambition and work in order to thrive.

In this chapter we unravel the wisdom behind God's plan for us to strive for growth and achievement. We discuss the difference between contentment and happiness. Together, we explore the delicate dance between ambition and greed and empower you to tune into the infinite potential within you.

It's time to discover new insights, challenge perspectives, and cultivate a mindset of boundless growth and happiness.

Exercise 2.1 Word Search Puzzle

Solve the following word search puzzle by finding words related to desires and ambition. Words may be found vertically or horizontally.

W	G	E	D	E	S	I	C	O	N	T	E	N
O	R	P	E	O	I	N	F	I	N	I	T	E
P	O	S	S	I	B	I	L	I	T	I	E	S
W	W	S	I	X	A	M	D	G	O	R	T	E
O	T	I	R	A	M	B	I	T	I	O	N	L
R	H	B	E	D	R	E	A	G	R	O	F	A
K	C	H	A	P	P	I	N	E	S	S	N	T

Words to Find

- *Ambition*
- *Desire*
- *Work*
- *Growth*
- *Happiness*
- *Infinite*
- *Possibilities*

Reflection

Exercise 2.2 Guided Reflection and Action Plan

Reflect on your desires and ambitions. Consider the areas of your life where you feel a longing for growth and expansion. What are your deepest aspirations and dreams? Write them down and connect with the infinite potential within you.

Exercise 2.3

Reflect on your understanding of the ideas of contentment versus happiness and the balance between rejoicing in what you have while also desiring more. Are there areas where you have settled for comfort instead of pursuing growth? Consider how happiness and ambition can coexist harmoniously in your life.

Exercise 2.4

Identify specific areas in your life where you should strive for growth and improvement. This could be in your career, relationships, personal development, or any other area that resonates with your desires. Write down the opportunities you see for expanding your world.

Exercise 2.5

Based on your reflections, set purposeful goals that align with your desires and ambitions. Develop a concrete action plan to support the achievement of your goals by breaking them down into smaller steps that move you closer to your desired outcomes.

Outline the steps you need to take, resources you may require, and any potential challenges you anticipate. Assign deadlines to your action steps and hold yourself accountable. A useful acronym to keep in mind as you plan your steps is SMART; your to-do list should be specific, measurable, achievable, relevant, and time bound.

Maintain consistent effort and commitment, even in the face of obstacles or setbacks. Stay motivated by reminding yourself of the infinite potential within you and the exciting possibilities that lie ahead.

Regularly reflect on your progress and assess whether you are moving closer to your desired outcomes. Celebrate your achievements and learn from any setbacks or challenges. Adjust your action plan as needed to stay aligned with your ambitions.

Remember!

You have been created in the image of an infinite God with incredible imagination, potential, and creative power.

Summary and Encouragement

In this chapter, we explore the profound concept that we are created in the image of an infinite God. We possess infinite imagination, potential, creative power, and desires. While God provided Adam with everything in the Garden of Eden, He also instilled in Adam the need to work and strive for more. Ambition is not a negative trait but a powerful motivator that drives us to do God's work and fulfill our purpose.

It is natural for our desires to evolve and grow as we progress through life. We should always be grateful for what we have, but that does not contradict our legitimate desire for more. We should never settle for complacency but instead welcome the infinite possibilities that lie ahead of us.

Secret #2 highlights the importance of both work and interdependence. Our fellow human beings' innate desire for more, as well as our own, fuels the functioning of society. By actively engaging in work, we contribute to the well-being of others and make life easier for one another. Our collective ambition and commitment to growth create a harmonious and thriving community.

Do not fear the target that constantly moves. It is a testament to our continuous growth and evolution. The exciting possibilities of the infinite can guide you toward innovation, progress, and fulfillment. Contentment should not be a limiting force. Instead, acknowledge the dynamic nature of your desires and aspirations. A content cow in a meadow is a beautiful sight, but as a human being, you are called to explore, create, and expand your horizons.

Knowing that we are created in the image of an infinite God should ignite a fire within us, reminding us that we possess boundless potential and creativity. God's will for us is to tap into our infinite potential and contribute to a world that reflects His glory.

Secret #3

Humans Alone Possess the Ability to Transform Themselves

Secret #3 prepares you to unlock the extraordinary power within you—the power to transform your life. Unlike animals, people possess the incredible ability to reinvent ourselves and rise above limitations.

This chapter explores the inspiring stories of individuals who defied odds and achieved greatness. We read about Richard LeMieux's journey from homelessness to success and see the resilience of Holocaust survivors who rebuilt their lives. Their experiences inspire us to know that change is possible for everyone.

Changing your life path isn't easy. It may require leaving your comfort zone and heading into the unknown. The essential lesson is that you have the power to shape your future. This workbook will guide you in harnessing your true potential.

Are you ready to continue on this journey? Let's dive in and discover the incredible possibilities that await you.

Exercise 3.1

Unscramble the jumbled letters after each statement to form words related to the key concepts discussed in this chapter.

1. Unlike animals, ______________ have the unique ability to transform themselves. (MSUNHA)
2. ______________ can be daunting, but it is essential for personal development. By being open to new possibilities, we can unlock our true potential and experience growth. (AGECNH)
3. The individuals showcased in this chapter faced significant ______________, but they refused to let adversity define them. Their stories teach us the importance of resilience, determination, and exemplify the belief that we can overcome obstacles. (EAGLECHNLS)
4. Change can be accompanied by ________ and reluctance, as seen in examples such as ending a friendship or transitioning from old industries to new technologies. (NIPA)
5. Painful acts of ___________, changing, or separating are catalysts for personal growth, societal advancement, and the development of human potential. (INKGRABE)
6. ______________ is rooted in self-reflection, self-improvement, and a willingness to explore new possibilities. (STARNATIONMORF)

Answers:

1. humans; 2. Change; 3. challenges; 4. pain; 5. breaking; 6. Transformation

Exercise 3.2 Future Vision

Imagine your ideal future self, five years from now. Create a vision board or visual representation of what this version of yourself looks like. Include various aspects of your life, such as finance, family, friendships, faith, and fitness. Use images, words, and symbols to depict your aspirations and goals.

Activity 3.3 Guided Reflection and Action Plan

Find a quiet and comfortable space where you can think without interruption. Close your eyes, take a deep breath, and let the words and ideas from the chapter settle within you.

1. Bring your awareness to the idea that as a human being, you possess the innate ability to transform yourself. Reflect on the stories shared in the chapter where individuals overcame great challenges and limitations to achieve remarkable personal growth and success. Recognize that you too have the power to shape your own destiny.
2. Reflect on a specific moment in your life when you experienced a significant period of personal growth. It could be a time when you overcame a fear, achieved a goal, or embraced a new perspective. Recollect the emotions, thoughts, and actions that accompanied this journey. Allow those memories to inspire and remind you of your capacity for change.
3. Take a moment to examine the different areas of your life where you desire growth. This could include relationships, such as family and friendship, your financial life, your spiritual and faith path, your fitness and health, or any other aspect that feels important to you.
4. Focus specifically on the financial aspects of your life. Contemplate whether, like Abraham and Moses, you have ever stepped forward without the reassurance that others were taking the same path. Are you ready to break from a mold to acquire greater wealth?

5. Set intentions for the changes you wish to make in those areas of your life. Identify specific actions, habits, or mindset shifts that align with your aspirations. Write these intentions down as a commitment to yourself.

6. Think about what potential challenges or obstacles might arise as you start on this path. Consider how you can proactively address and overcome these challenges. Cultivate a mindset of resilience, perseverance, and self-compassion, knowing that setbacks are a natural part of growth.

7. Imagine your future self, having successfully undergone the transformations you desire. Visualize yourself embodying the qualities, skills, and mindset that align with your aspirations. See yourself living a life of purpose, fulfillment, and joy. Allow this visualization to evoke positive emotions and a sense of empowerment.
8. Gently bring your awareness back to the present moment. Take a few deep breaths and let go of any remaining tension or thoughts. Carry the insights and intentions from this reflection with you as you move forward, knowing that you have the power to create the life you envision.

Remember!

Whenever you feel the need for guidance or inspiration, you can revisit this chapter. Making a new you takes dedicated and continuous work.

Summary and Encouragement

Unlike animals who remain bound to their inherent nature, humans possess a unique ability to transform themselves. The stories we shared exemplify the extraordinary results individuals can achieve.

Dennis Kimbro emphasizes in his book that wealth is not determined by birth or luck but by personal choice, commitment, discipline, self-improvement, and hard work. The remarkable success stories of Holocaust refugees, such as William Konar, Nathan Shapell, Jack Tramiel, Fred Kort, and Felix Zandman, highlight the indomitable spirit and resilience of the human soul.

These individuals overcame unimaginable horrors to achieve significant success and contribute philanthropically. Let them serve as an inspiration for you.

Embedded within Jewish culture is a belief in the inherent capacity for human growth. Biblical accounts, including those of Abraham and Moses, exemplify the power that choices we make have in reshaping our own destiny. There is always an invitation extended to improve our circumstances and step out of our comfort zones.

Just as the world shifted from horse-drawn carriages to automobiles, so too must we adapt to the ever-changing landscape of life. Know that the path may not always be smooth, but each step forward, no matter how small, brings you closer to your own improved future. Believe in yourself, for you possess the power to transcend, grow, and shape a life that surpasses your wildest dreams. You can achieve extraordinary heights.

Secret #4

The Universe Was Created for Connection

Let's look more deeply into Secret #4. In this chapter, we explore the profound truth that the universe thrives on connection. It's a reminder that we are not meant to journey alone. Our lives find meaning and fulfillment through deep and genuine connections with others. Furthermore, the more we connect with others, the better our financial outlook will be.

Think of those moments when you felt truly alive—the joy of shared laughter, the warmth of a heartfelt conversation, or the comfort of knowing someone truly understands you. These experiences reflect the essence of our existence—the need to connect with, support, and uplift one another.

But sometimes, we forget this fundamental truth, especially when it comes to our business lives. We get caught up in our own struggles and isolate ourselves, believing we can find success alone.

In this chapter, we discover the beauty of serving others and the impact it has on both us and those around us.

Exercise 4.1

Read each question carefully and choose the best answer from the options provided. Circle the letter corresponding to your chosen answer.

1. What do the authors use as an analogy to emphasize the importance of going with the natural flow of reality for success?
   a. Electricity and magnetism
   b. Gravity and inertia
   c. Light and sound
   d. Friction and pressure

2. According to this chapter, why is connecting with others and serving one another important?
   a. It is a way to gain power and control over others.
   b. It is a principle of human nature to be self-centered.
   c. It aligns with the natural laws of reality and leads to success.
   d. It is a religious obligation imposed by God.

3. What is the authors' stance on the relationship between monetary reward and virtuous service?
   a. Monetary rewards compromise the virtue of service.
   b. Virtuous service should always be done without any financial benefit.
   c. Monetary reward does not diminish the virtue of service.
   d. Virtuous service should be done secretly without anyone knowing.

4. How do the authors suggest that individuals can have a greater impact through philanthropy?
   a. By giving away money for free to those in need
   b. By using their business skills to create new businesses that serve customers, provide job opportunities, and stimulate the economy
   c. By focusing on distributing large sums of money quickly
   d. By donating money to traditional philanthropic bureaucracies

5. What is the significance of starting every column of the Torah with the letter "vav" (and)?

a. It symbolizes a specific commandment in the Torah.

b. It is a sign of grammatical correctness in Hebrew writing.

c. It highlights the interconnectedness and continuity of the Torah and the world.

d. It represents a break in the narrative of the biblical text.

Answers:

1. b; 2. c; 3. c; 4. b; 5. c

Exercise 4.2 Connection Reflection Walk

1. Go to a nearby park, garden, or any natural setting.
2. Contemplate the concept of connectivity presented in Secret #4.
3. Observe the interconnectedness of nature, such as how plants, animals, and ecosystems rely on each other to thrive.
4. During the walk, think about how your own connections with others impact your well-being and sense of purpose.
5. After the walk, share any insights or reflections that came to your mind during the experience.

Exercise 4.3 Guided Reflection

This activity is designed to help you embrace the power of connectivity in your life, inspired by the ideas presented in this chapter. Follow the steps below to explore the concept of connection and its potential impact on your well-being and success.

Step 1: Reflect on the Power of Connection

Consider the following questions:

1. How do you currently view and prioritize connections in your life, both personal and professional?
2. Have there been instances in your financial and business life when you experienced the positive effects of connecting with others?
3. Are there areas in your life where you feel a lack of connection and could benefit from fostering stronger bonds?

Step 2: Identify the Impact of Connection

Think about the ways in which embracing connectivity could positively impact various aspects of your life. Consider areas such as relationships, personal growth, finances, and overall well-being. Ask yourself the following questions:

1. How might deeper connections with others enhance your personal happiness, business success, and fulfillment?
2. How could building stronger networks and relationships benefit your career and professional opportunities?

3. What positive changes might you experience in your life by actively seeking meaningful connections?

Step 3: Recognize Barriers and Resistance

Examine any barriers or resistance you may have toward embracing deeper connections. These could be fear of vulnerability, past negative experiences, or a preference for solitude. Reflect on the following questions:

1. What factors or beliefs may be holding you back from actively seeking and nurturing connections?
2. How can you address these barriers and overcome resistance to open yourself up to more meaningful relationships?

Step 4: Set Connection Goals

Based on your reflections and insights, set specific connection goals that you would like to achieve. Consider both short-term and long-term goals related to your personal and professional relationships. Consider the following examples:

1. Strengthen existing friendships by scheduling regular meetups or virtual calls.
2. Expand your professional network by joining industry-related groups.

3. Take steps to overcome social anxiety and fear of rejection to connect more confidently with others.

Step 5: Develop an Action Plan

Create an action plan to help you achieve your connection goals. Break down each goal into actionable steps, set timelines, and identify resources or support you may need. Some examples of action steps could include the following:

1. Reach out to old friends or acquaintances to reconnect.
2. Research and sign up for social, charitable, and professional gatherings in your area or online.
3. Practice active listening and empathy in your interactions with others to strengthen your connections.
4. Seek a mentor in your area of specialization as well as look for someone whom you can mentor.

Remember!

The act of connecting with others is a natural and essential aspect of the human experience.

Summary and Encouragement

The universe was created for connection. When we go against the current of connection, our efforts often end in disappointment. Instead, the chapter encourages us to swim with the current, finding success and fulfillment by embracing its power.

The chapter raises the idea that creating a business can be an elevated form of philanthropy. As the adage goes, give a man a fish, and he eats for a day. Teach a man to fish, and he eats for a lifetime. Providing someone with the means to earn a living and provide for himself is greater than handing him what he needs. Using our resources to create more economic opportunity in the world is a source of joy. Release any notion that acquiring wealth from a profitable business diminishes its virtue. Instead, celebrate the interplay of connection and abundance.

See how blending and connecting ideas, resources, and talents can create powerful solutions and meaningful change. Let the examples shared inspire you to think creatively and explore new possibilities in your own life and endeavors. Appreciate the beauty of win-win situations, where both you and those you serve benefit.

Secret #5

Making Money Is a Spiritual Activity

In this chapter, we explore the extraordinary idea that making money isn't just about transactions; it's a profound spiritual experience.

Picture this: you exchange coins for something you desire, or perhaps, you sell something that another person desires. Two individuals, a buyer and a seller, are both happier because of the transaction. As we venture into the realm of commerce and spirituality, we discover the powerful connection between economic activities and our very souls.

Think about that moment when you worked tirelessly and, in doing so, made both a profit and improved someone else's life. It's not just about numbers; it's about recognizing the inner nobility of the voluntary exchange we call business.

Let us unravel the truth behind business and its spiritual essence. Together, we'll explore how economics can elevate us above the mundane and connect us with the God's plan for humanity. There is profound spirituality embedded within the world of making money!

Exercise 5.1

Read each statement carefully and determine if it is true or false based on the key concepts discussed in the chapter. Write "True" if the statement aligns with the ideas presented and "False" if it contradicts them.

_______________ 1. Economic transactions are purely physical actions and have no spiritual significance.

_______________ 2. The value of a currency is solely determined by how much precious metal it contains.

_______________ 3. Recognizing the spiritual nature of business helps individuals sync their careers with their greater life purpose and integrate moral values into their professional endeavors.

_______________ 4. Businesses can either make money or treat their employees correctly.

_______________ 5. Faith plays a significant role in commerce, as the value of money and the success of transactions rely on a belief in the future.

Answers:

1. False; 2. False; 3. True; 4. False; 5. True

Exercise 5.2 Spiritual or Physical?

Place each item in the following list under the category of "spiritual" or "physical." We may elevate physical acts to the spiritual, for example, by saying a blessing before eating and having meaningful conversation during the meal, but the act of eating itself is physical.

1. A violin
2. Reading
3. Loyalty
4. A mother protecting her child
5. A tune
6. Burials
7. Attacking a rival
8. Urinating
9. Setting a table with fine china
10. Selling one's product in exchange for dollar bills

Physical	Spiritual

Answers:

1. Physical; 2. Spiritual; 3. Spiritual; 4. Physical; 5. Spiritual; 6. Spiritual; 7. Physical; 8. Physical; 9. Spiritual; 10. Spiritual

Activity 5.3 Guided Reflection and Action Plan

Think about your personal journey and how your past experiences have shaped your perspective on money, work, and success. Consider significant milestones, both positive and challenging, that have impacted your understanding of financial matters.

Contemplate the spiritual aspects of your economic activities. Have you ever felt embarrassed at naming a price for your services? Do you suspect, perhaps deep inside you, that working for a nonprofit is intrinsically more noble than working for a profit-based business?

Think about your interactions with employees and customers. Do you prioritize their well-being and needs in your business or work environment?

Step 1: Shift Your Paradigm

Challenge conventional wisdom and consider the revolutionary idea that business is inherently spiritual. Recognize that the notion of business as a necessary evil is a misconception that undermines the true essence of commerce. Break free from these limiting beliefs and open your mind to the concept that business is a noble, moral, and dignified pursuit.

Step 2: Explore the Spiritual Spectrum

Engage with the concept that business lies on the spiritual end of the human activity spectrum. Reflect on how economic interactions involve faith, creativity, and intention. Consider the deeper layers beneath the exchange of coins, recognizing the powerful spiritual elements at play in every transaction. Understand that making money is not disconnected from your spiritual journey; it is an integral part of it.

Step 4: Reevaluate Your Beliefs

Reevaluate any preconceived notions you might have about business and its relation to spirituality. Challenge assumptions that associate business with greed or selfishness. Instead, recognize that conducting business ethically and creating value align with your inherent nobility as a human being.

Step 5: Reflect and Apply

Pause and reflect on your own experiences in business and how they line up with the principles explored in this chapter. Identify instances where you've contributed positively to others' lives through your business endeavors. Consider how your journey as a business professional integrates with your spiritual growth.

Step 6: Set Intentions

Define clear intentions for your future business activities. Embrace the idea that your economic pursuits are not separate from your spiritual path but rather are an intrinsic part of it. Commit to conducting business with integrity and a profound understanding of its spiritual dimensions.

Step 7: Embody the Spiritual Entrepreneur

As you continue your journey, strive to embody the essence of the spiritual entrepreneur. Recognize that your role involves not just financial success,

(*continued*)

but also contributing to the well-being of others. Make decisions that reflect the spiritual principles you've explored and inspire those around you to see the beauty of business in a new light.

Step 9: Integration and Transformation

As you implement the concepts from Secret #5 into your business endeavors, notice the transformation taking place within you and around you. Observe how your perspective shifts, your decisions match your spiritual values, and your sense of purpose deepens.

Remember!

Business is not just a monetary transaction; it is a spiritual expression. Every honest exchange is a testament to your inherent nobility and the value you bring to others. Success isn't a sign of greed; it's a manifestation of your ability to uplift and contribute to the world.

Summary and Encouragement

In this chapter, we explored the notion that making money is more than just a physical act; it is a spiritual activity. We examined the spectrum between spirituality and physicality, realizing that economic exchange, unlike eating or defecating, lies closer to the spiritual end.

When you engage in business transactions, you are participating in a spiritual dance of human connection and impact. Let your core values guide you toward decisions that align with your spiritual principles.

Your work should be a canvas for creativity and a means of making a difference in the world. Empower your employees, nurture a positive work environment, and always strive to make a positive impact on those around you.

As you walk this journey, let your spirituality shine through, and let your financial endeavors be a testament to your unique human abilities.

Secret #6

Everything Important and Joyful You Have Achieved Has Been in Partnership with at Least One Other Person

Secret #6 explores the profound power of partnership and how it shapes not only individual success but also entire industries. In this chapter, we dig into the realm of creativity, cooperation, and collaboration, and discover the biblical secrets that underpin successful living and entrepreneurship.

Partnership is a fundamental principle that reverberates through human endeavors. Every product or venture needs the feedback and involvement of others before it can reach its full potential. Business professionals rely on colleagues and customers alike to thrive, emphasizing the undeniable truth that success is built upon a foundation of partnership and community.

Throughout this chapter, we examine three key elements essential to the act of creation as demonstrated by the creation of a child. Firstly, creativity requires at least two people—cooperation and collaboration are at its core. Secondly, these people must be different from each other, bringing diverse perspectives and ideas that fuel innovation. And lastly, the importance of gratification deferred through hard work and perseverance leads to an act of creation that is profoundly satisfying and joyful.

The symbolism of bread, sacred in many faiths, further exemplifies the power of partnership. Bread serves as a reminder that when people come together, their collective creative capacity multiplies, enabling them to achieve great things that were impossible alone. We discover that true wealth lies in our connections with others, and we must approach them with warmth, respect, and the readiness to serve.

We unravel some biblical secrets that have shaped the successes of countless individuals and industries throughout time and space. As you progress through this chapter, keep in mind that every joyful and significant achievement in your life has been in partnership with at least one other person. Appreciate the power of partnership, and you will find yourself on a path to greater success and fulfillment.

Exercise 6.1

Match the key concepts with their corresponding definitions.

1. ____ Working together and achieving joy through collaboration

2. ____ A biblical metaphor for money

3. ____ Act of patience and hard work leading to the ultimate joy of accomplishment

4. ____ Different perspectives and strengths

5. ____ A mythical person

A. Diversity of thought and skills

B. Deferring gratification

C. Power of partnership

D. Bread

E. The totally independent, isolated creator

Answers:

1. C; 2. D; 3. B; 4. A; 5. E

Exercise 6.2 Partner Appreciation Letters

This exercise encourages gratitude for and reflection on the impact of those who participated in making you who you are today. Write a heartfelt letter of appreciation to someone who has been a significant factor in your achievements and joyful experiences. This is a worthwhile exercise even if for whatever reason you can't physically deliver the letter to the recipient.

Activity 6.3 Creative Partnership Vision Board

Create a vision board that represents your ideal partnerships and collaborative projects. Include images and words that inspire you to work together with others.

Activity 6.4 Guided Reflection and Action Plan

1. Think about various aspects of your life where collaboration has played a role, such as relationships, work, hobbies, or community involvement.
2. Take a moment to think about significant achievements or joyful experiences you have had in the past. These could be anything from personal milestones to professional accomplishments.

   Write down at least three achievements or experiences that stand out to you. For each achievement/experience, answer the following questions:

   - What was the specific achievement/experience?
   - Who were the people involved in making it happen (e.g., family members, friends, colleagues, mentors)?
   - How did other people contribute to the success or joy of the achievement/experience?
   - What did you accomplish from working together with others that you would not have been able to accomplish alone?

3. Identify three current partnerships in your life. These can include ongoing collaborations at work, community involvement, shared hobbies, or any other form of cooperation. List these current relationships and briefly describe each one, including its purpose and the people involved.

4. Consider the impact of these partnerships on your life and achievements. Then, answer the following questions:

   - How have these collaborations enriched your life and experiences?
   - In what ways have these alliances helped you overcome challenges and achieve your goals?
   - What skills or qualities have you developed through working with others?

5. Think about your future and the potential for new business partnerships and collaborations. Set some related goals for yourself, such as seeking out new connections, strengthening existing partnerships, or pursuing cooperative projects. Write down your goals and the steps you plan to take to achieve them.

Remember!

Lean into the power of partnership and collaboration. As you move forward, keep your heart open to new connections and diverse perspectives, for it is in these shared endeavors that true creativity blossoms.

Summary and Encouragement

This chapter reminds us that every significant achievement and joyful moment we have experienced has been in partnership with at least one other person. Whether in personal relationships or professional endeavors, working together with others is the driving force behind our accomplishments and moments of elation.

We recognize the value of diverse perspectives and strengths in enhancing creativity and problem-solving. The act of deferring gratification is also highlighted as a vital component of our journey toward ultimate joy and a sense of accomplishment.

Practice the art of deferring gratification, knowing that the journey toward your goal may be long, but the joy of accomplishment will be immeasurable.

Take this wisdom with you as you navigate both personal and professional endeavors. Cherish the partnerships that have shaped your past and be open to new connections that will enrich your future.

Secret #7

Focus on Other People's Needs and Desires, and You Will Never, Ever Be Short of What You Yourself Desire and Need

"Focus on Other People's Needs and Desires and You Will Never, Ever Be Short of What You Yourself Desire and Need" is a keen truth that people often leave out of the equation when choosing which areas of business to pursue.

We explore the parallel between the desire for physical intimacy and the pursuit of wealth. Just as God desires men and women to live in the sacred covenant of marriage, we discover that God also wants us to be preoccupied with one another's needs and wants. By serving each other selflessly, we open ourselves to the blessings of wealth and happiness.

Making money is not a selfish pursuit, nor is it something that should cause us to be ashamed. Instead, it is a dignified and moral activity that aligns with God's plan for us. Money is the consequence of serving others, not the ultimate goal. Our true purpose lies in connecting with one another, understanding each other's wants and needs, and serving each other honestly and transparently.

Throughout this chapter, we uncover the importance of meaningful connections and how being in proximity to others allows us to communicate, collaborate, and create. The more people who know us, like us, and trust us, the greater our chances of experiencing financial success and personal fulfillment.

As we explore the story of Cain and the lessons it holds, we discover the profound impact of appreciating others and how it enriches our lives in ways we cannot imagine.

Let this chapter be your guide as we look at the beautiful harmony inherent in serving others and reaping the rewards of wealth and joy that come naturally when we prioritize the needs and desires of those around us.

Exercise 7.1

Choose the correct answer for each question.

1. What is the main emphasis of the chapter?

  a. Focusing on fulfilling other people's needs and desires

  b. Accumulating personal wealth without considering others

  c. Pursuing personal desires above all else

2. Why, according to the chapter, can serving others lead to success?

  a. Serving others is a way to manipulate people for personal gain.

  b. God built a system that rewards those who serve others.

  c. Serving others ensures no competition in the market.

3. What does the biblical account of Cain and Abel teach us in the context of serving others?

  a. Other people are obstacles to our own success and wealth.

  b. We should see the Bible as a history book or as literature.

  c. We should view other people as allies rather than as competitors.

4. How can creating meaningful connections with others benefit us?

  a. It helps us gang up against competitors and gain a monopoly in the market.

  b. It allows opportunities to explore mutually profitable exchanges.

  c. It can't. Creating connections is solely for personal gain.

5. How does the chapter view the relationship between money and serving others?

  a. Money is the consequence of serving others.

  b. Money is the primary goal, and serving others is a means to achieve it.

  c. Serving others is essential, but money is not a direct result of it.

6. Why do businesses and industries often cluster together in specific areas?

  a. To avoid competition and monopolize the market.

  b. Proximity allows for better communication and collaboration.

  c. City planners force businesses and industries to stay in one place.

7. According to the chapter, why is understanding human needs crucial for financial success?

a. It helps us manipulate and exploit people for personal gain.

b. Understanding needs enables us to provide desired goods and services.

c. Knowing needs is irrelevant as long as marketing is effective.

8. What is part of the formula for financial success, as stated in the chapter?

a. Pursuing personal desires relentlessly

b. Accumulating wealth without considering others

c. Focusing on serving God's other children

Answers:

1. a; 2. b; 3. c; 4. b; 5. a; 6. b; 7. b; 8. c

Exercise 7.2 The "Needs and Desires" Survey

1. Create a simple survey with questions related to the needs and desires of your family, friends, or colleagues.
2. Ask them to participate in the survey, either in person or through an online form.
3. Collect the responses and analyze the data to identify common themes and areas where you can potentially provide help or solutions.
4. Reflect on the insights gained from the survey.

Activity 7.3 Create Your "Service Offering" Portfolio

1. Review your skills, passions, and expertise from the workbook exercises in previous chapters.
2. Create a "Service Offering" portfolio that showcases how you can serve others through your talents.
3. Include examples of how your skills can address various needs and desires in your community or workplace.
4. Share your portfolio with friends, family, or potential clients to let them know how you can be of service to them.

Activity 7.4 Guided Reflection and Action Plan

1. Reflect on the key concepts presented in the chapter. Consider how these concepts relate to your own life, values, and beliefs. Use the following questions to guide your reflection:
   - How do you currently approach the idea of serving others in your personal and professional life?
   - Have you ever experienced moments when focusing on serving others led to positive outcomes or unexpected rewards?
   - In what ways do you think fulfilling other people's needs and desires can impact your own success and happiness?

(*continued*)

After reflecting on the key concepts, create an action plan to implement the principles of service and success in your life. Consider the following steps:

1. Discover Needs and Desires: Take time to understand the needs and desires of people around you. Engage in conversations and actively listen. When friends and family express frustration, ask yourself how their lives might be made easier in that specific area. Empathize with others to better understand how you can be of service.
2. Build Meaningful Connections: Seek to build authentic and meaningful connections with others, both personally and professionally. Focus on developing relationships based on trust, respect, and mutual support.
3. Foster Collaboration: Look for opportunities to collaborate with others, whether in your workplace, community, or social circles. Collaboration can lead to new ideas, innovation, and increase your positive impact on others.

Remember!

The journey to incorporating the concept of service into your life is ongoing. It requires commitment, patience, and a genuine desire to positively impact the lives of others. By serving and collaborating, you can create a fulfilling and rewarding life that benefits both you and those around you.

Summary and Encouragement

This chapter emphasizes the profound connection between serving others and achieving personal success and fulfillment. It presents the idea that just as God desires men and women to marry and live in loving, committed unions, He also wants us to be genuinely preoccupied with meeting the needs and desires of our fellow human beings. The chapter continues to refute the notion that making money is purely a self-centered pursuit and instead asserts that earning a living is a noble act that creates

happiness for others through providing goods and services that fulfill their wants and needs.

The concept of service is highlighted as the key to unlocking both spiritual happiness and financial prosperity. By focusing on serving other people and establishing meaningful connections with others, we create a ripple effect of positive impact on ourselves and those around us. The chapter stresses the value of human connection and collaboration, demonstrating that clustering with others in a community or industry can lead to increased opportunities for success.

In your pursuit of success, let the principle of service guide you. Contribute to the happiness and well-being of others, and trust that by doing so, you will contribute toward your business success as well.

Secret #8

Become a People Person

In Secret #8, "Become a People Person," we look at how to practically utilize the power of human connections that are essential to achieving success, happiness, and prosperity in both your personal and professional life.

The chapter opens with a thought-provoking comparison between IQ and CQ. While intelligence is important, it is not the sole, or the best, determinant of success and happiness. Very highly intelligent individuals may struggle with building social networks, which can hinder their ability to thrive financially and socially.

The core principle of this chapter is that we, as human beings, are wired for connection. Throughout history, the power of human interconnectedness has driven economic expansions and breakthroughs, leading to unprecedented prosperity. The Bible itself emphasizes the importance of connections, declaring, "It is not good for man to be alone."

Viewing yourself as a businessperson, regardless of your profession or role, is a key point. Understanding that your employer is essentially your main customer changes the way you approach your work. A sense of ownership creates an entirely different work atmosphere.

Connecting with other people is not always easy, especially for those who consider themselves shy or introverted. However, we explore how personal growth and change are not only possible but necessary. Through practice, you can improve your facial expressions and body language, making it easier for others to connect with you authentically.

In the following workbook activities, reflections, and assessments, you will have the opportunity to internalize and apply the principles of Secret #8. By developing your people skills and fostering meaningful connections, you will discover a whole new world of opportunities and fulfillment waiting for you. Create a future of prosperity and happiness through the power of being a people person!

Exercise 8.1

Test your understanding of the key concepts from Secret #8, "Become a People Person." Fill in the blanks with the correct answer for each question.

1. People with a high CQ (connectivity quotient) are likely to have many friends and large professional and social networks, which is positively correlated with __________, health, and wealth.
2. Your employer is your __________. Adopting this mindset will lead you to approach your tasks in an entirely different way.
3. The key to successful exchange and collaboration lies in celebrating our __________ as human beings, allowing us to trade knowledge, wisdom, and skills.
4. The more __________ you have, the greater your chances of meeting the people who can change your personal and professional life.
5. Making your face more __________ and animated can improve your ability to connect with others effectively.

Answers:

1. happiness; 2. customer; 3. differences; 4. connections; 5. expressive

Exercise 8.2 Meet and Greet

1. Find an opportunity to attend a social gathering or community activity.
2. Approach at least three new people and introduce yourself with a warm smile.
3. Be aware of social nuances and your counterpart's body language. A warm handshake can be a friendly gesture, or it could be an intrusion.
4. Ask other people about themselves and actively listen to their responses.
5. Look for common interests or experiences that you can discuss.
6. Share a brief introduction about yourself, including your name and profession, touching on your areas of commonality.
7. Use tips and techniques to remember people's names and something about them.
8. Exchange contact information if appropriate.
9. After the event, challenge yourself to list as many as possible of the names of and bits of information about those you met as you can remember.

Activity 8.3 Facial Expression Challenge

1. Stand in front of a mirror or use a camera to record yourself.
2. Practice different facial expressions, such as smiling, showing concern, surprise, and attentiveness.
3. Pay attention to how your face conveys different emotions and how you can improve your expressions.
4. Record a short video or take a photo of yourself demonstrating your most engaging facial expression.
5. Share the video or photo with a trusted friend or mentor and ask for his or her feedback and suggestions.
6. Practice regularly until you feel more comfortable and natural with your improved expressions.

Activity 8.4 Become Comfortable with Diversity of Thought and Experience

1. Take some time to think about the diverse range of people you interact with regularly, both personally and professionally.
2. Identify three individuals who have different backgrounds, interests, or perspectives from you.
3. Reach out to these individuals and initiate a conversation to learn more about their experiences and ideas.
4. Listen actively to what they are saying.

5. Reflect on how their unique qualities and insights can enhance your own personal growth and broaden your understanding of the world.
6. Write down your reflections and consider how you can continue to enlarge your world through your interactions and relationships.

Activity 8.5 Guided Reflection and Action Plan

1. Think about your current interactions with others, both personally and professionally. Do you actively seek new connections and opportunities to expand your network, or do you find yourself sticking to familiar circles? Consider the range of people you interact with and whether you are open to connecting with many types of individuals.
2. Evaluate your networking skills and identify areas where you feel confident and areas that may need improvement. Do you have an approachable and engaging demeanor? Are you actively listening to others during conversations? Assess how well you convey interest and sincerity through your facial expressions and body language.
3. Reflect on the importance of connection in various aspects of your life, such as personal relationships, professional opportunities, and overall well-being. Consider the benefits of having a strong network of friends, colleagues, mentors, and collaborators.

(*continued*)

Action Plan

1. Pursue New Opportunities: Commit to seeking out new opportunities for networking and connection. Participate in community activities that align with your interests and goals. Be open to meeting new people and engaging in meaningful conversations.
2. Improve Your Facial Expressions: Practice improving your facial expressions to convey interest and sincerity. Stand in front of a mirror or use a camera to record yourself practicing various expressions, such as smiling, showing concern, and attentiveness. Seek feedback from others and make regular practice a part of your routine.
3. Embrace Different Groups and Experiences: Seek out individuals with different backgrounds, experiences, and perspectives. Engage in conversations with them, actively listening and learning from their insights. This will broaden your horizons and enrich your understanding of the world.
4. Set Networking Goals: Develop specific networking goals that align with your personal and professional aspirations. Determine the number of new connections you want to make within a defined period and the types of relationships you want to build. Create a timeline for achieving these goals and set actionable steps to get there.
5. Monitor Your Progress: Regularly take note of your progress in becoming a people person. Take note of the connections you've made, the insights you've gained, and the impact on your personal and professional life. Celebrate your successes and identify areas for improvement. Be willing to adjust your approach and continue growing as a people person.

Remember!

Becoming a people person is a journey that requires effort, patience, and a genuine interest in connecting with others. By actively engaging in reaching out and improving your communication skills, you will enhance your ability to build meaningful relationships and open doors to new opportunities in both your personal and professional life.

Summary and Encouragement

This chapter stresses the importance of face-to-face connections and genuine interactions. It highlights the value of being open to meeting people from different backgrounds, providing new opportunities for growth and collaboration. The ability to effectively communicate, show interest, and express sincerity through facial expressions plays a pivotal role in becoming a successful people person.

Becoming a people person is not just a skill; it is a mindset and a way of life that can transform your personal and professional journey. Recognize that building a strong network of friends, mentors, and colleagues will enrich your life in countless ways.

Every individual you meet is someone to whom you can contribute and who has something valuable to offer you, and every connection you make can open doors to new opportunities. Cultivate the art of networking and make a genuine effort to connect with others. By doing so, you will not only enhance your own life but also become a positive force in the lives of those around you.

Put on a warm smile and welcome the incredible possibilities that lie ahead on your path to becoming a people person.

Secret #9

We Love the People Whom We Help More Than We Love Those Who Help Us

Secret #9 of our journey through ancient Jewish wisdom explores a fascinating principle that accentuates the power of human connections and the dynamics of love and reciprocity. This secret delves into the profound truth that we tend to love and feel more connected to those for whom we do acts of kindness than those who do favors for us.

In this chapter, we encounter a story of a judge who, by offering shelter to a stranger during a rainy day, found himself facing a profound moral dilemma in the courtroom. This tale serves as an introduction to the concept that doing a favor for someone creates a unique bond that goes beyond mere gratitude. We explore how this principle applies not only to personal relationships, such as parent-child dynamics, but also to business relationships and our overall social interactions.

Throughout this workbook chapter, you will travel on a journey of self-reflection and exploration of your own relationships. You will discover the significance of investing in others and, perhaps more importantly, allowing others to invest in you. You will encounter the challenges of receiving favors and the transformative effects of helping and being helped. By understanding this biblical business secret, you will gain insights into building strong, meaningful connections with others and unlocking the potential for greater success and happiness in both your personal and professional life.

Exercise 9.1

Unscramble the jumbled words after each statement to find the key concepts related to the chapter.

______________________ 1. The state of being interconnected with others, which is crucial for personal and professional growth (VINTONECYCT)

______________________ 2. The feeling of thankfulness and appreciation for the kindness or help received from others (DEARGUTIT)

______________________ 3. A word that describes an area where similar businesses set up near to each other (URCELST)

______________________ 4. One way that children can help the family unit flourish (RCEHSO)

______________________ 5. The natural but unworthy feeling that we tend to experience when others have provided valuable assistance (SEEERTTNM)

Answers:

1. Connectivity; 2. Gratitude; 3. Cluster; 4. Chores; 5. Resentment

Exercise 9.2 Interview with a Helper

1. Identify a person who has helped you in a meaningful way.
2. Conduct an interview with this person, asking questions about their motivations for helping and how it made them feel.
3. Write down your realizations and what you have learned from this activity.

Activity 9.3 Reflection Journal

1. Recall an instance where you went out of your way to help someone.
2. Write about your feelings and emotions during that situation.
3. Did you feel more connected or invested in the person you helped?
4. Write your reflections on ways you can increase your interconnectedness with others based on the chapter's teachings.

Activity 9.4 Guided Reflection and Action Plan

1. Reflect on favors you have performed for others in the past. How did these acts make you feel? Did you notice any changes in your emotions or attitude toward the recipients?
2. Think about the times when others have helped you or shown kindness to you. How did you feel when receiving help? Did you feel more connected to those who assisted you or to those you assisted?
3. Take a moment to evaluate your relationships with family, friends, and colleagues. Are there specific individuals whom you have helped or who have helped you? How do you perceive these relationships compared to others?
4. Look for patterns in your behavior and emotions related to giving and receiving help. Do you find it easier to show kindness to others or to accept help from them? Are there specific situations or contexts that influence your feelings?

Action Plan

1. Practice Acts of Kindness: Challenge yourself to perform at least one act of kindness each day for someone else. It could be a simple gesture, such as holding the door for a stranger, complimenting a colleague's work, or reaching out to someone going through a tough time. Record your experiences and emotions associated with each act of kindness.
2. Express Gratitude: Express gratitude and appreciation to one person who has helped you in the past. Write a thank-you note or call or meet up with them to let them know how much their support meant to you.
3. Foster Relationships: Build stronger connections with others. Seek opportunities to spend time with family and friends, engage in activities together, and provide support when needed. Remember that investing in relationships leads to deeper bonds and feelings of connectedness.
4. Reciprocate Help: When someone aids you, receive their help graciously. Remember the principle that accepting help leads to stronger connections and a sense of balance in relationships. If someone helps you, look for opportunities to reciprocate or pay it forward.
5. Reflect on Resentment: If you find yourself feeling resentful or uncomfortable after receiving help from someone, take a moment to explore the reasons behind these emotions. Reflect on any underlying beliefs or attitudes that may be influencing your response.
6. Practice Empathy: Put yourself in the shoes of others when they offer help or act kindly toward you. Consider what might be their motives and feelings, recognizing that they may experience the same sense of connectedness and love when helping as you do.
7. Community Involvement: Engage in community service or volunteer work to help others outside your immediate circle. Participate in activities that align with your passions and interests, as this can lead to a deeper sense of fulfillment and interconnectedness with your community.
8. Challenge Negative Narratives: If you notice negative narratives or feelings of entitlement creeping in when someone helps you, challenge these thoughts. Remind yourself that receiving an act of kindness is a privilege.

(*continued*)

9. Share Experiences: Discuss your reflections and action plan with friends, family, or a support group. Sharing your journey and insights can provide encouragement and inspire others.
10. Continuously Reflect and Adjust: Regularly assess your progress in making new friends and connections. Adjust your strategy as needed.

Remember!

Nurturing relationships by both receiving favors and delivering them leads to a more fulfilling and connected life. By understanding the biblical business secret that we feel closer to those we help, we can form and grow relationships with those around us.

Summary and Encouragement

The chapter explores the powerful principle of human psychology that reveals how assisting others creates a deep bond and connection with them. Ancient Jewish wisdom offers valuable insights into understanding this phenomenon, showing that we tend to feel more affection and attachment to those we help than to those who help us.

Additionally, the chapter emphasizes the importance of gratitude and reciprocation, as expressing appreciation and repaying favors can deepen relationships and foster a sense of balance in interactions. By nurturing interconnectedness through acts of kindness and by strengthening our powers of empathy, we build stronger personal and professional networks, ultimately leading to a more enriched life.

Be open to receiving help from others with grace and appreciation. Remember that accepting help allows others to experience the joy of giving, strengthening the bond between you and fostering a sense of interconnectedness.

Practice gratitude and reciprocation in your relationships. Express appreciation to those who have assisted you and seek opportunities to return the favor or pay it forward to others. By doing so, you can create a cycle of connection and warmth that enriches your life and builds your business.

Secret #10

Life Isn't About What You Know—It's About Who You Are

Contrary to popular belief, merely possessing information does not guarantee positive outcomes. Society often misleads us into thinking that knowledge can fix all our issues. We were promised, for example, that ensuring that people knew the dangers of smoking would end the popularity of cigarettes. However, as we lay out in this chapter, these assumptions are often flawed. Many of the challenges we face are not due to a lack of knowledge but rather to a failure to act in alignment with what we already know. True transformation and achievement come from building the strength of our characters and consistently making the right decisions.

Knowledge alone cannot alter behavior; it requires the development of our character. We may be fully aware of what needs to be done to succeed in various aspects of life, whether it's maintaining good health, achieving financial success, or excelling in our careers. However, translating that knowledge into consistent action is where the real challenge lies.

Throughout this chapter, we explore the significance of making the right decisions and taking ownership of our characters. Success and fulfillment come from welcoming the wisdom of ancient teachings and integrating them into our daily lives.

Let us remember that the key lies not just in knowing what to do, but in understanding the context and internalizing these valuable principles. By integrating these concepts into our lives and developing the character necessary to act upon them, we can create positive change and reach new heights of personal and professional achievement.

Exercise 10.1

Determine whether each statement is true or false based on the key concept discussed in this chapter. Write "True" if the statement aligns with the chapter's message and "False" if it does not.

____________________ 1. Society often believes that knowledge alone can solve all problems.

____________________ 2. Criminals commit crimes because they lack information.

____________________ 3. Knowledge of the dangers of smoking has led to the eradication of smoking.

____________________ 4. Knowledge alone can alter our behavior and lead to better choices.

____________________ 5. The Ten Commandments in Exodus and Deuteronomy are identical.

____________________ 6. The Fourth Commandment in Exodus reads, "Guard the Sabbath Day."

____________________ 7. Internalizing God's word and acting upon it is crucial to building character.

____________________ 8. To succeed, we must know what actions to take, not necessarily understanding the idea in a larger context.

____________________ 9. The concept of "the square root of negative one" has no use in mathematics.

____________________ 10. Integrating ancient Jewish wisdom into our lives can lead us to change our behaviors.

Answers:

1. True; 2. False; 3. False; 4. False; 5. False; 6. False; 7. True; 8. False; 9. False; 10. True

Exercise 10.2 Character Traits Assessment

Following is a character traits assessment tool consisting of various statements. Read each statement carefully and rate yourself on a scale of 1 to 5, where 1 = Strongly Disagree and 5 = Strongly Agree. Be honest in your responses. Once you have completed the assessment, analyze your results, and identify areas for improvement.

Items	Strongly Disagree 1	Disagree 2	Neutral 3	Agree 4	Strongly Agree 5
1. I consistently act in alignment with my core values and beliefs.					
2. I take responsibility for my actions and choices, both positive and negative.					
3. I am committed to personal and professional growth and development.					
4. I make decisions based on principle rather than short-term gains.					
5. I am open to learning from others and hearing different perspectives.					
6. I actively seek opportunities to improve my character and moral compass.					

(continued)

Items	Strongly Disagree 1	Disagree 2	Neutral 3	Agree 4	Strongly Agree 5
7. I exhibit resilience in the face of challenges and setbacks.					
8. I strive to be honest and transparent in my interactions with others.					
9. I practice self-discipline and resist temptation when necessary.					
10. I show empathy and compassion toward others' feelings and experiences.					
11. I demonstrate integrity by keeping my promises and being trustworthy.					
12. I seek opportunities to contribute positively to the well-being of others.					
13. I actively practice self-reflection and take ownership of my flaws.					

Items	Strongly Disagree 1	Disagree 2	Neutral 3	Agree 4	Strongly Agree 5
14. I am patient and understanding when dealing with difficult situations or people.					
15. I show humility and easily admit when I am wrong.					
16. I handle conflicts with grace and aim for win-win solutions.					
17. I demonstrate self-control in managing my emotions and reactions.					
18. I am diligent and persistent in pursuing my goals and aspirations.					
19. I hold myself accountable for the impact of my actions on others.					
20. I exhibit gratitude and appreciation for the blessings in my life.					
TOTAL SCORE					

Scoring

- Add up your scores for all the statements.
- The highest possible score is 100 (5 points for each statement).
- The lowest possible score is 20 (1 point for each statement).

Analysis

- If your total score is between 80 and 100, you exhibit strong character traits and are committed to personal growth. Identify areas where you can continue to improve and be a role model for others.
- If your total score is between 60 and 79, you have several positive character traits but have room for improvement. Focus on enhancing your character to become a more well-rounded individual.
- If your total score is below 60, there are opportunities for significant growth in your character traits. Work on becoming the best version of yourself.

Reflection

1. Write down your overall assessment score and any insights you gained from the assessment.
2. Identify the character traits where you scored high and reflect on how you can continue to nurture and build upon those strengths.
3. Identify the character traits where you scored low and think of ways to work on improving in those areas.
4. Set specific goals and action plans for character development.
5. Align your goals with your core values.

Activity 10.3 Guided Reflection and Action Plan

Take some time to reflect on the key concepts from this chapter, "Life Isn't About What You Know—It's About Who You Are." Consider the following questions and write down your responses:

1. How has society's belief that knowledge can solve all problems affected your own perspectives and actions?
2. Can you recall any instances where you relied solely on knowledge but still faced challenges in your personal or professional life?
3. How do you perceive the relationship between knowledge and behavior in your own experiences?
4. Have you ever found it challenging to channel what you know into consistent actions? If so, what were the obstacles?
5. In what ways do you believe building your character can contribute to your making better choices and decisions?

Action Plan

Step 1: Prioritize Character Development

Choose one or two character traits you want to focus on developing further. These should be traits that you believe will have the most significant positive impact on your life and the lives of those around you.

Step 2: Set Specific Actionable Goals

Create specific, measurable, achievable, relevant, and time-bound (SMART) goals related to character development. For example, if you want to work on patience, examine what situations cause you to be impatient and make a plan for dealing with those situations.

Step 3: Create a Daily Routine

Integrate your character development goals into your daily routine. Allocate time each day to work on these traits, such as through mindfulness exercises, journaling, or setting specific hours where you will be most cognizant of that trait.

Step 4: Seek Support and Accountability

Share your action plan with a trusted friend, family member, or mentor. Having someone to support and hold you accountable will increase your chances of staying committed to your character development journey.

Step 5: Practice Self-Reflection

Challenge yourself to fill in a "report card" before going to bed for a specified number of days. Record your progress—and failures—in developing the chosen character traits. Be honest with yourself about your successes and areas where you can improve. Use setbacks as learning opportunities and remain committed to growth.

Step 6: Celebrate Progress

Acknowledge and celebrate the positive changes you observe in yourself as you work on character development. Celebrating milestones, no matter how small, will reinforce your commitment to the process.

Remember!

Character development is a lifelong pursuit. Foster personal and professional growth that will lead you to become the best version of yourself.

Summary and Encouragement

"Life Isn't About What You Know—It's About Who You Are" challenges the prevailing notion that knowledge alone can solve all problems. Instead, it emphasizes the significance of character development and aligning personal values with goals. The chapter highlights that knowing what to do is insufficient; real progress comes from integrating that knowledge into consistent actions that reflect one's core values.

Don't be disheartened by past struggles to convert knowledge into action; instead, see them as opportunities for growth. Focus on a few character traits you wish to strengthen and work diligently toward embodying them in your interactions and decisions. Recognize that self-improvement is a journey, and every step, no matter how small, contributes to your growth.

Secret #11

In Order to Achieve Success, We Must and Can Build Up Our Self-discipline, Integrity, and Strength of Character

In this chapter, we delve into the importance of self-discipline, integrity, and character in achieving success. We explore how these virtues serve as powerful motivators, guiding us toward our goals and aspirations.

Imagine embarking on a journey to lose weight or achieve financial success. We are often faced with conflicting desires—the immediate pleasure of indulging in tempting foods or activities versus the long-term benefits of a healthier lifestyle or financial stability. Our minds tend to prioritize immediate relief, making it challenging to stay committed to our long-term goals.

The secret to overcoming this struggle lies in aligning our actions with our values and strengthening our character to resist temptation and make positive choices. The ancient wisdom of the book of Psalms, particularly Psalm 34:13, offers valuable guidance on the path to self-improvement.

Throughout this chapter, you will learn that celebrating small victories and setting actionable goals are powerful techniques to cultivate self-discipline and integrity. You are encouraged to create a personal board of directors—trusted individuals who will hold you accountable and support you on your journey.

Success in business and life depends not only on knowledge but on the ability to act with moral conviction. As human beings, we have the capacity for change and improvement, and this chapter shows you how to stay true to your goals. As you grow and strengthen your character, you will find it easier to make choices aligned with your aspirations.

Exercise 11.1

Solve the following word search puzzle by finding words that represent steps toward realizing your dreams and making progress on your journey. Words may read vertically or horizontally.

A	C	C	O	U	N	T	A	B	I	L	I	T	Y
V	S	S	U	S	U	C	C	E	S	S	L	E	G
A	E	M	A	C	C	O	G	R	O	W	T	H	A
L	L	O	V	A	L	U	G	R	O	W	T	P	I
U	F	R	C	H	A	R	A	C	T	E	R	A	N
E	D	A	V	L	E	A	D	E	R	S	H	I	P
S	E	L	F	D	I	S	C	I	P	L	I	N	E

Words to Find

- *Self-discipline*
- *Moral*
- *Gain*
- *Pain*
- *Success*
- *Growth*
- *Leadership*
- *Accountability*
- *Character*
- *Values*

Exercise 11.2 Character Traits Assessment

For each question, select the answer that best represents your typical behavior or response in the given situation. Be honest with yourself as you go through the assessment. Remember, this is not about judgment but about understanding yourself better and identifying areas for personal growth.

1. When faced with a difficult task or challenge, I tend to

a. procrastinate and avoid it as long as possible.

b. break it down into smaller steps and tackle it systematically.

c. seek help from others to handle it for me.

2. How do you prioritize your commitments and responsibilities?

a. I often prioritize short-term gratification over long-term goals.

b. I prioritize based on what aligns with my core values and long-term objectives.

c. I tend to be inconsistent in prioritizing my commitments.

3. When things don't go as planned, I

a. blame others or external circumstances for the outcome.

b. learn from the experience and adapt my approach.

c. get discouraged and give up easily.

4. How do you handle ethical dilemmas or situations that challenge your integrity?

a. I sometimes compromise my values to avoid conflict or gain an advantage.

b. I stay true to my values, even if it means facing difficulties or setbacks.

c. I sometimes take the easy path of going with the majority, without thinking about the issue.

5. How do you respond to criticism or negative feedback?

a. I become defensive and avoid accepting responsibility for my actions.

b. I take feedback as an opportunity for growth and use it constructively.

c. I get demotivated and feel inadequate when receiving criticism.

6. When pursuing a long-term goal, how do you maintain focus and motivation?
    a. I often lose sight of my goals and get distracted easily.
    b. I regularly review my progress and remind myself of the reasons for pursuing the goal.
    c. I rely on external rewards or praise to keep me motivated.
7. In challenging situations, how do you handle stress and pressure?
    a. I tend to react emotionally.
    b. I stay composed and try to find constructive solutions to cope with the stress.
    c. I avoid confronting difficult situations.
8. How do you handle setbacks or failures?
    a. I tend to blame external factors and avoid taking responsibility for the failure.
    b. I view failures as learning opportunities and use them to improve.
    c. I dwell on my mistakes and let them discourage me from trying again.
9. How do you approach commitments and promises you make to others?
    a. I frequently break commitments.
    b. I take commitments seriously and do my best to honor my promises.
    c. I often make promises impulsively and struggle to follow through.
10. When faced with a moral dilemma, how do you decide what to do?
    a. I prioritize my personal interests or gains over ethical considerations.
    b. I carefully weigh the consequences and implications of each option on my values.
    c. I let others make the decision for me or follow the crowd.

YOUR ANSWER	A	B	C
1			
2			
3			
4			
5			
6			
7			
8			
9			
10			
TOTAL POINTS			

Scoring

Assign the following points for each answer:

a. –1 point

b. +2 points

c. 0 points

Interpretation

- Total points less than 10: Note the opportunities for improvement in building positive character traits. Pick one area on which to work.
- Total points between 10 and 20: You have a balanced approach to character development. Strive to acquire more positive traits.
- Total points 20: You exhibit strong character traits. Review these questions periodically to make sure you are staying strong.

Activity 11.3 Guided Reflection and Action Plan

Take some time to think about the key concepts discussed in this chapter, including self-discipline, integrity, and perseverance. Consider how these character traits play a crucial role in achieving success and personal growth in various aspects of life. Think about your own experiences and behaviors related to these traits and be honest with yourself during this reflection process.

1. Self-Discipline: Consider times when you lacked self-discipline and how it affected your progress toward goals. Be alert for moments when you demonstrate self-discipline and notice positive outcomes.
2. Integrity: Examine situations in which you faced ethical dilemmas and how you handled them. Look back on instances when you compromised your values and the impact it had on your self-respect and relationships.
3. Perseverance: Think about challenging circumstances where you showed perseverance and how it helped you overcome obstacles. Contemplates times when you gave up too easily and missed opportunities as a result.

Write down your reflections in the space provided:

Action Plan

It's time to create an action plan to strengthen and further develop positive character traits. Follow these steps:

1. Set Clear Goals: Define achievable goals related to self-discipline, integrity, and perseverance. Write them down and be specific about what you want to accomplish.

2. Identify Triggers and Challenges: Recognize situations or triggers that often lead you to act against your best character.
   a. These moments are often unavoidable such as being stuck in traffic.
3. Develop Strategies: Plan not only how to grit your teeth and face these times, but how to turn them into positive occasions, for example, by listening to a podcast.
   a. In the previous example of traffic, shout "Yes!" the next time you are sitting still. Rather than stewing, express gratitude for this opportunity to test yourself. (Really!)
4. Celebrate Small Victories: Acknowledge and celebrate every small success in developing positive character traits. Recognize that progress is a journey and each step counts.
5. Learn from Setbacks: Failures or setbacks are learning opportunities. Analyze what went wrong and plan for how you can respond differently in the future.
6. Continuous Learning: Seek out books and articles or listen to podcasts that focus on character development and personal growth.

Remember!

Building strong character traits is an ongoing process that requires dedication and self-awareness. Every step you take toward strengthening these traits brings you closer to achieving success in all areas of your life. Your character is the foundation for achieving your goals and becoming the person you aspire to be.

Summary and Encouragement

While we may have infinite desires and ambitions, our character traits are a determining factor in whether we turn those aspirations into reality. Self-discipline helps us resist immediate temptation in pursuit of long-term goals, integrity ensures that we make ethical choices, and perseverance enables us to overcome setbacks on our journey toward success.

Cultivate self-discipline by making small, positive choices every day that align with your long-term goals. Hold yourself accountable for your actions and learn from any setbacks you encounter. Value integrity as the foundation of trust and respect in all relationships, both personal and professional. Perseverance is the key to overcoming obstacles and turning setbacks into stepping stones. By cultivating self-discipline, integrity, and perseverance, you can unlock your full potential and lead a fulfilling and purpose-driven life.

Secret #12

Your Authentic Identity Requires Other People

We develop our identity through intentional relationships with other people. While most of us crave solitude on a regular basis, and we may think best without anyone nearby, we need contact with other people to test our ideas and aspirations. We may prioritize, for example, staying calm no matter the provocation, but until we are provoked, we do not know that we can do so.

By choosing our business partners and colleagues wisely, we watch how other people act in various situations. This makes it easier for us to emulate them. Our relationships are a key to discovering our true selves and realizing our ambitions.

Exercise 12.1

Navigate through a series of twists and turns that represent the journey of pursuing your dreams and ambitions relentlessly. Your goal is to spell out the title of this chapter and reach the end of the maze.

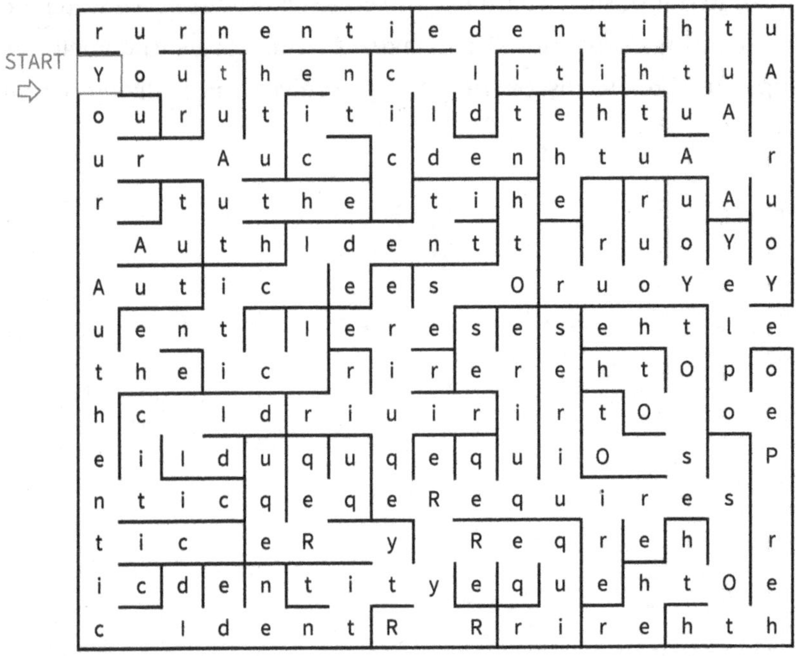

Answer

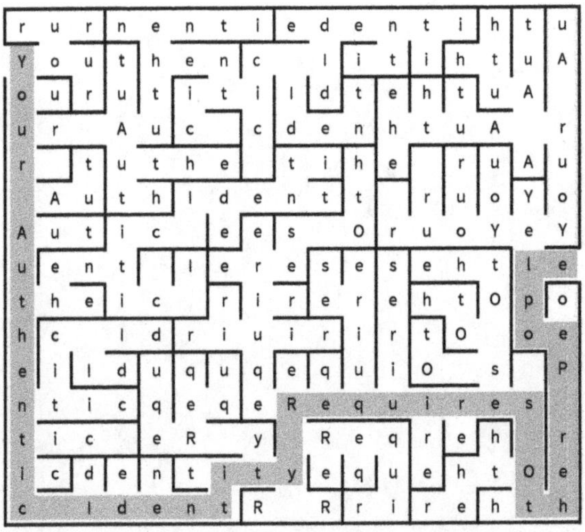

Exercise 12.2 My Identity Map

Create a personalized identity map showing the connections that have shaped you.

1. Draw a large circle in the center of a blank page and write "My Authentic Identity" inside it.
2. Surround the circle with smaller circles representing the people in your life. Various circles might have your parents' or teachers' names, those of neighbors or customers, your spouse, or your children. For each one, place a description in the large circle defining yourself as a son/daughter, student/teacher, etc.

Activity 12.3 Identifying Meaningful Connections

- Think about three individuals in your life who play or played a significant role in shaping who you are today.
- Write down the names of these people and the specific traits or qualities that you admire in them.
- Have you modeled your behavior on theirs? What specific areas did you choose to emulate?

Activity 12.4 Guided Reflection and Action Plan

Consider the following questions:

1. Do you behave differently depending on whom you are with?
2. Does this reveal an appropriate and valid understanding of different types of relationships, or is it due to a lack of having a core identity? Review those relationships and ask yourself which it is.
3. How often do you change your way of thinking or acting after discussing it with others?
4. How do you define authenticity, and how do you ensure you stay true to yourself as you interact with others?
5. Have you ever felt isolated or disconnected, and if so, how did it affect your sense of identity?
6. Did governmental or personal imposed isolation during COVID-19 change you because you were distanced from many people in your life? In what ways?

Write down your reflection in the space provided:

Action Plan

Create a practical action plan based on insights from the chapter.

1. Cultivate Self-Awareness:
   - Identify relationships that inhibit you from being true to your vision of yourself.
   - Reassess those relationships.
2. Seek Meaningful Connections:
   - Actively reach out and connect with individuals who share similar values.
3. Stop yourself from building a business structure or theoretical ideas only in your imagination. Test them by involving other people.

Remember!

Building an authentic identity requires continuous effort and openness to the influence of others. As you develop connections and relationships, you will discover new facets of yourself and evolve a deeper sense of purpose and fulfillment in your personal and professional life.

Summary and Encouragement

Secret #12, "Your Authentic Identity Requires Other People," emphasizes the significance of connections and relationships in shaping our authentic identity. We benefit from connecting with others as we build our character and sense of self.

The story of Adam in the Garden of Eden illustrates the transformative power of relationships. Only after connecting with Eve does Adam's full identity emerge. We define ourselves through our interactions with others.

Secret #13

Know How Business Works; Understand Specialization and Cooperation

Business is often misunderstood, with many believing it to be inherently exploitative. This misguided notion arises from a lack of knowledge about how business truly operates. This chapter seeks to dispel these misconceptions and shed light on the real essence of business.

Language shapes culture, mindset, and business practices. By understanding how language affects our perception of money and wealth, we gain valuable insights into how the language in which we think may help or hinder us in becoming successful in business.

Reviewing the significance of collaboration in business and how it fosters interdependence and unity among individuals helps us to appreciate the spiritual aspects of business, recognizing that ethical capitalism aligns with God's desire for human connectivity and prosperity.

Throughout this workbook, we encourage you to reflect on your own experiences and observations regarding business and economics. Engage with the thought-provoking questions and exercises provided to internalize these concepts and apply them to your own professional journey.

Exercise 13.1 Crossword Puzzle

Fill in the crossword puzzle with the key concepts related to the chapter, "Know How Business Works; Understand Specialization and Cooperation." Read the clues carefully to find the correct words. Each key concept corresponds to a unique definition.

Crossword Puzzle

Across

3. The achievement of predetermined goals, objectives, or desired outcomes, often measured by the fulfillment of personal, professional, or financial aspirations
4. The shared beliefs, values, customs, traditions, language, and behaviors of a particular group of people that influence its way of life and interactions
6. The unique characteristics, traits, and qualities that define an individual or group, shaping their sense of self and influencing how they interact with others and the world around them

7. An economic system based on private ownership of resources and businesses, driven by market forces of supply and demand, where individuals and companies aim to generate profits
8. The process of working together, pooling resources, and sharing ideas, expertise, or responsibilities to achieve common goals and maximize productivity and creativity
9. The process of focusing on and developing expertise in a specific area or skill, allowing individuals or entities to become more efficient and productive in their respective fields
10. The study of how individuals, societies, and nations allocate resources, make choices, and interact within markets to produce, distribute, and consume goods and services to satisfy their needs and wants

Down

1. The confidence and reliance placed in someone's integrity, character, and ability to fulfill commitments, resulting in a sense of security and dependability in relationships and interactions
2. The practice of engaging in economic activities, trade, and commerce to create, produce, and exchange goods or services for profit or mutual benefit
5. The overall perception and evaluation of an individual, organization, or brand based on their past actions, conduct, and performance, which influences trust and credibility

Answers:

Crossword Puzzle

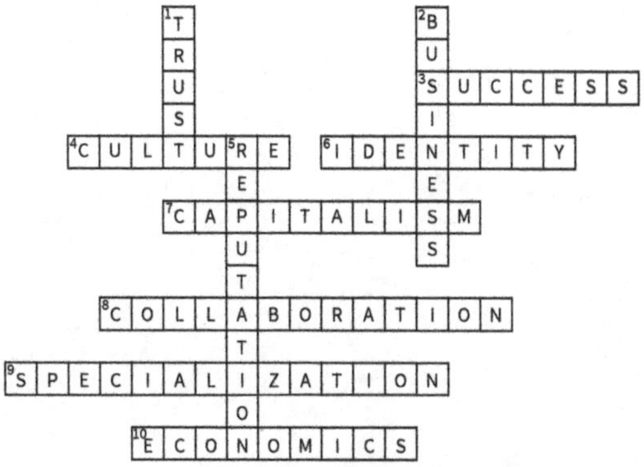

Exercise 13.2 Case Study Analysis—Warren Buffett and Business Reputation

1. Read again the part of the chapter that discusses how Warren Buffett was brought in to save Salomon Brothers.
2. Research and gather more information about Buffett's role in saving Salomon Brothers.
3. Create a case study analysis that explains how Buffett's reputation and expertise influenced the outcome of the situation at Salomon Brothers.
4. Discuss the importance of competence and reputation in the business world, using this case as an example.

5. A negative rumor about your business starts spreading on social media, threatening your reputation. You suspect a rival company might be behind it. How might you respond to protect your reputation without engaging in negative tactics?

Activity 13.3 Winning Versus Earning

1. Does your native language distinguish between winning money and earning money?
2. Do you participate in games of chance and lotteries?
3. Why do you think that lotteries have earned the nickname, "a tax on the foolish"?

4. Does gaining insight into the idea that language plays a role in shaping our perspectives on earning versus winning money carry implications for you?

5. What is your perception of business leaders and their earnings? Can you name more famous actors, outstanding athletes, or business leaders?

Action Plan

1. Add to your reading list some of the books mentioned in this chapter as well as others that relate to business.
2. Monitor your given language for any lingering incorrect or negative words and phrases about money and business. Write them down, and then stop using those words. Work on reframing your perspective.

(*continued*)

3. If there are highly paid people in your company whose function you do not understand, take the time to research what they do. It is possible that they are employed for the wrong reasons, but it is more likely that they provide valuable services that bring in more than their salary.

Remember!

Use this newfound knowledge and self-awareness to shape your business journey and work toward your entrepreneurial goals with confidence and purpose.

Summary and Encouragement

This chapter emphasizes the importance of understanding how business works and the role of specialization and cooperation in economic success. The chapter challenges the misconception that business is inherently unfair and driven by greed. It highlights the significance of culture and language in shaping economic attitudes and behaviors.

We explore the concept of earning versus winning money in different languages. While some languages distinguish between the two, Hebrew, the Lord's language, only has a word for earning. This linguistic insight reflects a cultural perspective that values mutually beneficial transactions over zero-sum games.

Drawing on examples from history and biblical references, this chapter illustrates how specialization allows individuals and communities to thrive by recognizing their unique strengths and then trading goods and services.

Furthermore, the chapter acknowledges that unethical practices can exist in business but urges everyone not to let these instances deter them from pursuing success through ethical capitalism and collaboration.

Embrace the concept of earning money through transparent transactions, where both parties benefit. Recognize that collaboration and specialization are keys to prosperity, just as they were in the examples provided. Remember that ethical capitalism promotes shared success.

Secret #14

Every One of Us Is a Business Professional

Secret #14, "Every One of Us Is a Business Professional," emphasizes the importance of embracing a professional mindset. Regardless of what you do, you are a business professional responsible for your own success.

This chapter analyzes the key concepts of being a true professional in your field. Promptness, dedicating oneself to work, and the power of loving what you do are important takeaways. Develop an understanding of what it means to act like a business professional and how to apply these principles to achieve success and fulfillment.

In today's competitive world, it's crucial to recognize that we are all in business, whether as entrepreneurs, employees, freelancers, or any other role where we trade services or products for financial gain. The legitimacy of being a business professional is not bestowed upon us by external entities; it's a mindset we adopt and embody. By investing in our work, committing to our business goals, and serving others with excellence, we develop a genuine love for what we do. Being a true professional doesn't mean staying busy; it means prioritizing and executing tasks that align with your goals and responsibilities.

Exercise 14.1

Match the key concepts with their corresponding definitions.

1. ____ Someone who does only what he loves doing

2. ____ One who trade services or products for financial gain

3. ____ The Latin root of *amateur*, which means "to love"

4. ____ The Hebrew for "to work it"

5. ____ The quality of performing one's work with dedication, promptness, and a commitment to excellence.

A. Le-Ovdah

B. Amor

C. Professionalism

D. Amateur

E. Business professional

Answers:

1. D; 2. E; 3. B; 4. A; 5. C

Exercise 14.2 "Professional Superhero" Visualization

Superheroes have been a staple of the entertainment industry since being introduced in the 1930s. While X-ray vision, the ability to become invisible, and warrior powers may be alluring, it is time to focus on the new and exciting "professional superhero."

If you are artistically inclined, draw this superhero. If that strength isn't in your toolbox, write a description of this superhero.

Activity 14.3 Guided Reflection and Action Plan

- Do you see yourself as a business professional, or do you tend to downplay your significance?
- Analyze your actions and behaviors in the workplace or when conducting business. Are you prompt, reliable, and committed to doing what needs to be done?
- Are there times that you have prioritized personal interests over professional responsibilities? Does this occur frequently?
- Acknowledge areas where you could improve your professionalism, such as time management, communication, or taking initiative.
- Anticipate how acting like a business professional will enhance your reputation, build trust with others, and open new opportunities.

Action Plan

1. Set Clear Professional Goals:
    - Define specific, measurable, achievable, relevant, and time-bound (SMART) goals related to your professional growth.
    - Break down your goals into smaller milestones to track your progress.
2. Practice Promptness and Accountability:
    - Keep a record of your tasks. Write down when you plan to tackle them and how long each task should take. Track how accurate your expectations are and, if you missed your deadlines, why that happened.
    - Set reminders or use time management techniques to stay on track with deadlines.

3. Foster a Positive and Supportive Work Environment:
   - Encourage a culture of professionalism and mutual respect among colleagues and team members. Being around coworkers who slack off is debilitating.
   - Lead by example, treating those around you as professionals.

Remember!

Being a business professional is not limited to specific job titles or industries; it is a mindset and a way of approaching your work and interactions with others. Take deliberate steps toward becoming the best version of yourself as a business professional.

Summary and Encouragement

This chapter emphasizes the importance of viewing ourselves as business professionals and acting as such. We must adopt a professional mindset and approach in all aspects of our work and interactions. Being a business professional goes beyond mere job titles; it is about taking responsibility, being reliable, and doing what needs to be done promptly.

Take pride in your work and commit to doing what needs to be done, when it needs to be done. Your reliability and promptness will set you apart and earn you respect and trust from colleagues, employees, and superiors alike.

When you dedicate yourself to your work, you will find yourself loving your work. This genuine passion will fuel your success and satisfaction.

Secret #15

Develop Four Dimensions of Your Life Simultaneously

Secret #15 recounts the vital concept of balancing all aspects of our lives to achieve true success and fulfillment. This chapter reminds us that life is multidimensional, and it is essential to nourish every aspect simultaneously to lead a meaningful and prosperous life.

It is crucial to recognize that we are not defined solely by our work. We are complex beings with physical and spiritual needs that interconnect and impact one another. Neglecting any sector of our lives can lead to imbalance and dissatisfaction.

We lay out the four dimensions of life and how they are interconnected. Neglecting any one of them leads to an unbalanced life. By addressing all four dimensions simultaneously, we create a harmonious and well-rounded existence, allowing us to thrive both personally and professionally.

Exercise 15.1

Please read each question carefully and select the best answer from the choices provided. Each question has only one correct answer. Choose the option that you believe best aligns with the key concepts discussed in this chapter.

1. What is the key distinction between physical and spiritual needs?

a. Physical needs are essential for survival, while spiritual needs are optional.

b. Physical needs can be measured in a laboratory, while spiritual needs cannot.

c. Physical needs are always tangible, while spiritual needs are intangible.

d. Physical needs are universal, while spiritual needs vary from person to person.

2. What is the significance of the ladder as it relates to the word *SH-L-M* in Hebrew?

a. The ladder symbolizes physical needs, and *SH-L-M* represents spiritual needs.

b. The ladder represents spiritual needs, and *SH-L-M* stands for physical needs.

c. The ladder signifies climbing toward completion.

d. The ladder represents career growth, and *SH-L-M* symbolizes financial security.

3. Which quadrant in the four-dimensional matrix represents physical needs supplied by the world physically?

a. Upper-left quadrant

b. Lower-left quadrant

c. Upper-right quadrant

d. Lower-right quadrant

4. What can happen when we neglect our spiritual needs?

a. We will experience immediate physical harm.

b. It will not have any impact on our overall well-being.

c. We relinquish all religious affiliation.

d. Neglecting spiritual needs can lead to physical and financial distress.

5. Why do the authors caution against having a one-dimensional view of life?
   a. It leads to despondency and failure.
   b. It makes people lazy.
   c. It prevents people from focusing on their careers.
   d. It hinders comprehensive growth.
6. What can be considered a spiritual need fulfilled by something physical?
   a. Faith and spirituality
   b. Emotional connections with friends
   c. Financial security and investments
   d. Survival necessities like food and water
7. Which statement best describes the relationship between professional success and personal well-being?
   a. Personal well-being depends entirely on professional success.
   b. Personal and professional lives have no impact on each other.
   c. Personal well-being is a distraction and should be ignored for professional growth.
   d. Success can contribute to personal well-being and vice versa.
8. How do spiritual needs influence our physical well-being?
   a. Spiritual needs have no impact on our physical well-being.
   b. Fulfilling spiritual needs means you will never get sick.
   c. Spiritual connections affect our mental and emotional health, which in turn impacts our physical health.
   d. Fulfilling spiritual needs guarantees financial security.
9. What is the main takeaway from the chapter regarding work and personal life balance?
   a. Focus solely on professional growth and ignore personal needs.
   b. Neglecting personal life has no negative consequences for professional life.
   c. Personal life should be prioritized over professional growth.
   d. Balance and develop all aspects of life simultaneously for true success and fulfillment.

10. What role does making money play in fulfilling spiritual needs?

a. Making money is irrelevant to fulfilling spiritual needs.

b. Making money is the only way to fulfill spiritual needs.

c. Making money prevents individuals from focusing on their spiritual needs.

d. Making money provides spiritual satisfaction in knowing that we improved the lives of others.

Answers:

1. b; 2. c; 3. a; 4. d; 5. d; 6.c; 7.d; 8.c; 9. d; 10. d

Exercise 15.2 Balanced Life Chart

1. Use the provided template to create a Balanced Life Chart.
2. In each quadrant, list specific examples of physical and spiritual needs based on the concepts from the chapter.

Physical needs that the world supplies physically	Physical needs that the world supplies spiritually
Spiritual needs that the world supplies physically	Spiritual needs that the world supplies spiritually

Activity 15.3 Reflection

1. Examine the chart and consider how well you are currently meeting each need in both physical and spiritual ways.
2. Identify areas where you may be neglecting certain needs and explore how you can improve the balance in your life.
3. Think about the impact of fulfilling both physical and spiritual needs on your overall well-being and success in personal and professional aspects of life.
4. Expand your vision to include a larger time period than just the present. Ask yourself the previous questions over a five-year period and a ten-year period. When you picture the next five years, does it include all four dimensions?

Activity 15.4 Action Plan

1. Set Priorities and Goals:
   - Prioritize the needs that require immediate attention.
   - Set specific and achievable goals for meeting those needs, both physical and spiritual.
2. Create a Daily/Weekly Routine:
   - Allocate time for essential physical needs, such as proper nutrition, exercise, and sufficient sleep.
   - Dedicate time for spiritual practices, like meditation, prayer, or increasing your knowledge of the world.

Remember!

Achieving balance in all areas of your life is an ongoing process. Work toward creating a harmonious and enriching life that encompasses both your physical and spiritual needs.

Summary and Encouragement

In this chapter, we learn about the importance of developing all four dimensions of our lives simultaneously, including both physical and spiritual aspects. While the focus of this book is on professional development, it does not mean neglecting other crucial aspects of life, such as family, friendships, faith, and fitness.

The chapter emphasizes four dimensions in which constant growth is necessary for a harmonious life. As seen through the Hebrew word *S-L-M* leading to the word *SH-L-M*, all aspects of our lives must be complete and well developed. Neglecting one area while focusing solely on another can lead to imbalances and a sense of dissatisfaction.

Personal and professional growth go hand in hand. By nourishing both your physical and spiritual needs, you will cultivate a life filled with joy, purpose, and success.

Secret #16

Serve Authentically

In a world where we often come across individuals who seem to be more successful than we are, it's natural, albeit wrong, to feel a sense of envy or desire when looking at the accomplishments—and bank accounts—of others. This chapter urges us to shift our focus away from what others have achieved and concentrate instead on how we can serve our fellow human beings.

The quest for finding our true calling and purpose is common, especially for those entering or leaving college and starting their careers. Many advisors advocate "follow your passion" as the ultimate career advice. This chapter challenges that notion, asserting that true success lies not in seeking to do what we love but rather in finding what others need and dedicating ourselves to meeting those needs.

As you study this chapter, remember that genuine conviction and authenticity are crucial in our journey to success. People can discern when we are committed to our work and when we are merely seeking personal gain. Our focus should not be on financial gain but on serving others wholeheartedly, with a commitment to making a positive impact on their lives.

With this mindset, let us unpack Secret #16.

Exercise 16.1

Please read each question carefully and select the best answer from the choices provided. Each question has only one correct answer. Choose the option that you believe best aligns with the key concepts discussed in this chapter.

1. The key principle underlying personal wealth in this chapter is _______________ others faithfully and effectively.

2. Wealth is the ___________ of doing the right things and serving others, not the focus itself.

3. True success and prosperity come from investing ourselves wholeheartedly in our work and being _____________ in our commitment to serving others.

4. Earnings and profits are a result of forming _______________ and serving others faithfully.

5. The foundation on which the economy is built is fulfilling the _____________ of others.

Answers:

1. serving; 2. consequence; 3. authentic; 4. relationships; 5. needs

Activity 16.2 Self-serving or Authentic Serving?

Almost every career path can be followed in a way that is selfish or in a way that is dedicated to serving others. For each of the listed professions, write a sentence describing the mindset of someone pursuing it for the wrong reasons and then another individual pursuing it for the right reasons.

- Physician
- Clothing salesperson
- Social worker
- Financial counselor

Exercise 16.3 The Interview

Your mission is to get a job offer. Of course, before accepting it, you will want to review the compensation and benefits package. But those should not be at the top of your mind when you interview. Pick the best answer to each of the following questions.

1. Why do you want to work at *Sinks for You*?

- **a.** I play with a band in the evenings, and your store closes at 5 p.m.
- **b.** I am impressed with your reputation and know that you recommend the best fixtures for each customer. I love the idea of helping people get high-quality fixtures with the look that they want at the price they can afford.
- **c.** I hear that the commission is really high on each sale.

2. Why do you want to teach ninth-grade English?

- **a.** I love the idea of having the whole summer off. By the time you add in vacation and sick days, I can travel for a lot of the year.
- **b.** So many kids view reading as a school chore and writing as something to be avoided. I want to open their eyes to the magic of books and communication. The English skills they learn in ninth grade can change their lives.
- **c.** Well, I don't begin to understand algebra, but after all, I know how to read.

3. How did you become interested in this position?

- **a.** Someone mentioned that this is a great place to meet girls/guys.
- **b.** The blog post that your president shared on LinkedIn about . . . grabbed my attention. The more I read about what you do and your future goals, I became convinced that I could make a difference by working here.
- **c.** I don't remember. What exactly do you do?

Answer key: We are not providing one. You can figure this out for yourself. If you have trouble, please start reading the book from the beginning again.

Action Plan

Create a personalized action plan for integrating a service mindset into your career. Follow these steps:

1. Market Analysis: Research and identify areas in your field where there may be unmet needs or opportunities to serve others more effectively.
2. Skill Development: If necessary, outline any skills you may need to enhance or acquire to better serve others in your career.
3. Service: Describe how your desired field can be properly used or misused.
4. Authenticity and Conviction: Cultivate authenticity and a deep conviction for serving others in your career.
5. Professionalism and Dedication: Find ways to demonstrate professionalism and wholehearted dedication in your work.
6. Avoiding Envy: Focus on living your life, not on casting a jealous eye on the lives of others.

Remember!

Your authentic self will come across to those you encounter.

Summary and Encouragement

Wealth should not be our primary focus, but rather, the consequence of doing what is right—serving our fellow human beings. By embracing a service mindset and genuinely meeting the needs and desires of others, we create a foundation for success in both our careers and lives.

The key to achieving true fulfillment and prosperity lies in wholeheartedly committing ourselves to serving others. As you embark on your career journey, remember that success comes from genuine service and not from mere pursuit of personal gain. Take the time to reflect on how your strengths, skills, and abilities can be utilized to uplift and meet the needs of those around you.

Avoid falling into the trap of envy or focusing solely on your passions. Instead, focus on finding opportunities where your unique contributions can bring value to others. Cultivate authenticity and conviction in your work, knowing that people can recognize and appreciate genuine service.

Secret #17

Enhance Your Potential by Imposing Boundaries and Structure

In Secret #17 of our journey through *Business Secrets from the Bible* we uncover a profound insight that relates to many parts of our lives, including business. We investigate the importance of boundaries and structure.

We may read articles telling us that limitless freedom is the path to true liberation. Yet, paradoxically, it is by confining ourselves and establishing structure that we unlock genuine freedom and productivity.

In this workbook, we will explore the idea that by imposing limits and focusing on specific actions, we gain the power to achieve our goals and create true value in our lives and businesses. We will strive to align our actions with purpose, avoid distractions, and nurture the discipline needed for success.

Let's begin!

Exercise 17.1

Steven Spielberg's mother, Leah, spoke about allowing her young son to activate the kitchen blender without the lid to see what would happen. Not surprisingly, the result was a mess on the walls and ceiling. His upbringing may have helped the budding director to become successful in his future work, but let's face it, most of us aren't built in either his or his mother's mold. We would end up with the mess without a positive side effect.

Have fun with this exercise and think of five items in your life that would not be effective if there were no boundaries and structure. We offer a blender to start you off.

1. Making a smoothie in a blender without using a lid.
2.
3.
4.
5.
6.

Exercise 17.2 Prioritize Your Commitments

Identify and prioritize your current commitments to focus on those with the most significant impact on your goals and well-being.

- Write down all your current commitments and responsibilities, both personal and professional.
- Evaluate each commitment's importance and its alignment with your long-term goals.
- Assess the impact of each commitment on your life, career, relationships, and personal growth.
- Determine which commitments are nonnegotiable and crucial for your well-being and success.
- Consider the time and effort required for each commitment and how it affects your overall schedule.
- Reflect on your long-term aspirations and values to ensure your commitments align with your vision.
- Select the top commitments that contribute significantly to your goals and happiness.
- Review commitments that have a lower impact and consider delegating or letting go of some.
- Communicate your decision to de-prioritize or delegate commitments to relevant parties.
- Be open to adjustments in your priorities as circumstances change, but always keep your long-term objectives in mind.

Activity 17.3 Guided Reflection and Action Plan

- Reflect on your childhood and the boundaries that were imposed on you by parents or caregivers. Consider the impact these limits had on your understanding of rules and structure.
- Examine your current perception of limits, rules, and structure in your life. Do you see them as restrictive or liberating? How do they affect your productivity and creativity?
- Contemplate the paradoxical idea that setting limits and boundaries can lead to greater freedom and creativity. Identify instances in your life where you experienced this effect.
- Evaluate areas in your life where you struggle to impose limits or structure. Are there areas where you could benefit from more discipline and focus?
- Consider the relationship between freedom and direction. Reflect on times when focusing your energies on specific goals resulted in more significant achievements and personal growth.

Notes

Aha Moments! Did any part of this exercise lead you to understand your current behavior in light of your past?

Action Plan

1. Identify Goals and Priorities: Clearly define your personal and professional goals. Prioritize them based on their importance.
2. Establish Boundaries: Set specific boundaries and rules that align with your goals. Create a daily schedule that allows for focused and productive work, as well as time for growth and relaxation.

3. Use Time Management Techniques: Commit to effective time management practices. Use calendars, planners, or digital tools to track your commitments and progress toward your goals.
4. Limit Distractions: Identify common distractions in your daily life and find ways to minimize or eliminate them. This might include turning off notifications, setting specific work hours, or creating a designated workspace.
5. Accountability Journal: Track your daily accomplishments and progress toward your goals. Be honest with yourself about how you spend your time and whether you stay focused on your priorities.
6. Learn from Times When You Said, "No": Think of the occasions when you turned down an offer, opportunity, or invitation, only to discover that doing so allowed you the latitude to achieve other goals you did not anticipate.
7. Seek Support and Guidance: Reach out to mentors, coaches, or experienced individuals who can provide valuable insights and guidance on imposing effective boundaries and structures in your life.
8. Celebrate Successes: Recognize the positive impact of setting boundaries and staying committed to your goals.
9. Adapt and Refine: Be flexible in adjusting your boundaries and structures as needed. Life circumstances may change, and your priorities may shift, so be willing to adapt your approach accordingly.
10. Foster Creativity and Productivity: Understand that by accepting limitations and structure, you create the foundation for greater creativity and productivity. Appreciate the focus and clarity that boundaries provide to unlock your full potential.

Remember!

Imposing boundaries and structures in your life is not about limiting your potential but empowering yourself to achieve your goals. Welcome the paradox of freedom through limitation and let the power of discipline and direction lead you to greater success and fulfillment.

Summary and Encouragement

Secret #17, "Enhance Your Potential by Imposing Boundaries and Structure," emphasizes the importance of setting explicit boundaries and limitations to achieve true freedom and success. Drawing parallels from the way parents impose rules on their children to keep them safe and help them to accomplish goals, the chapter argues that adults also need to establish rules and structures to enhance productivity and creativity. By directing our energies and setting clear goals, we can accomplish great things and avoid the trap of unlimited freedom that leads to inefficiency.

As you venture through life's journey, remember the invaluable lesson from this chapter: freedom lies within boundaries; you must safeguard your own success by defining limits. It may feel counterintuitive at first, but by engraving your schedule in stone, you'll find the true freedom to be creative and productive.

Do not be afraid to limit your options, for it is within these boundaries that your real potential truly flourishes. Take a step back when overwhelmed, seek counsel, and simplify your perspective to conquer even the most complex challenges.

In your pursuit of success, commit to time management, and hold yourself accountable for meeting your goals. Be honest with yourself about your efforts and be brave enough to adjust your schedule or set more realistic objectives. True freedom is not the opportunity to do as you please but the chance to lock yourself into the things that truly matter.

Celebrate the power of limitation, and let it drive you toward your dreams.

Secret #18

You Cannot Lead If You Cannot Follow

A vital aspect necessary for workplace success often goes overlooked—the ability to accept authority. In the workforce, being able to take orders and respect authority are essential traits that open doors to success and growth.

Unfortunately, the educational systems through schools and universities often neglect teaching crucial life skills. Many students graduate without a proper understanding of how to be a team player, hindering their chances of securing and retaining jobs. At the same, they graduate without learning how to think and instead are trained to parrot what they are told. Many employers seek good character and the right attitude. Given those two attributes, they can train skills.

In this chapter, we learn the significance of accepting authority and the invaluable lessons it brings. Service is not just about performing tasks; it is about understanding the art of customer service and humility. True leaders recognize that they are always in service, whether to customers, stockholders, or employees.

Seek mentors, learn from others' experiences, and practice genuine service in your daily interactions. Just as Nordstrom's executives were expected to start from the sales floor, giving them a taste of proper customer service, you too can internalize the power of serving others.

Exercise 18.1

The following cryptogram is a message in substitution code. Each letter is substituted for a different one consistently through the quotation. For example, CAT might be spelled PRQ if every P stood for a C, every R stood for an A, and every Q stood for a T. (That is not the code for this sentence.) These words about working hard and well are followed by the author's name. Look for repeated letters, patterns, and common words.

"KJL XLYK EULECUCKQPZ MPU OPPF NPUT KPSPUUPN AY KP RP OPPF NPUT KPRCB" —LAXLUK JFXXCUR

Code: A = L; B = M; C = A; D = F; E = P; F = U; G = O; H = J; J = H; K= T; L = E; M = F; N = W; O = G ; P = O; Q = I; R = D; S = M; T = K U = R; V = Y; W = C; X = B; Y = S; Z = N.

Full quote and author name: The best preparation for good work tomorrow is to do good work today. —Elbert Hubbard

Exercise 18.2 Leadership Reflection

Answer the following questions based on your own schooling and experiences:

- Were you encouraged to recognize a hierarchy and show respect for those above you in rank, such as parents and teachers?
- Was your education based on training you only to parrot back what you were you expected to think critically?
- Have you held any entry-level jobs?
- Were you ever promoted from an entry-level job?

- Think about a leader who has inspired you. What qualities did he or she possess that made them an effective leader?
- When have you had the opportunity to serve others in a leadership role? Was it clear to those who followed you that there was someone above you as well?

Activity 18.3 Guided Reflection and Action Plan

- Are you comfortable undertaking any job that is needed in the workplace and in your personal life?
- Are there any tasks that you see as beneath you?
- How well do you handle being told what to do?
- Consider the leaders you admire. How do they demonstrate the balance between leading and serving others?
- Does your cultural background influence your views on authority and service?
- Do you consider yourself to have a "can-do" attitude at work?

Activity 18.4 Job Interview

Whether or not you are planning to interview for a position soon, prepare for an interview. List three questions you would formulate to ask at the interview. Make sure that these questions focus on showing what you can bring to the job rather than on what the job does for you.

Remember!

We grow into positions of authority. Before you try to lead others, be sure that you are capable of following a good leader.

Summary and Encouragement

The ability to serve others and accept authority is essential for success in the workplace and life. Current Western educational systems often fail to instill both the crucial skill of taking orders as well as that of thinking independently. A positive attitude and willingness to serve, as well as critical thinking skills, are highly valued by employers, often more than specific skills or qualifications.

Following orders and serving others doesn't mean surrendering your autonomy or self-respect; it signifies humility, respect for others, and the desire to contribute positively. As you journey through life and your career, remember these key points:

- Serve with enthusiasm.
- Seek mentors.
- Lead by example.

Cultivate an environment of collaboration, respect, and growth. True leadership is not about asserting dominance, but about inspiring and uplifting those around you.

Secret #19

Vision Is Necessary; Sharing That Vision Is Not Always Necessary

"Vision Is Necessary; Sharing That Vision Is Not Always Necessary" sheds light on the multifaceted nature of our lives and the importance of discretion in our interactions with others.

In the Hebrew language, the word for *face* is *panim,* a plural word, signifying that there are multiple facets to our being. Just as we have different faces that we present to different people in our lives, our inner thoughts and emotions are also varied. Not everyone needs to be privy to all aspects of our inner world.

Throughout this chapter, we work to understand the notion of multiple faces. They do not necessarily signal dishonesty, but rather they can be key aspects of moving through the world and maintaining healthy relationships. Just as successful leaders carefully select what information to share with their teams, we too must learn the art of discretion to navigate both personal and professional spheres effectively.

Moreover, we explore the art of active listening, as the words and vocal cues people use often reveal more than they intend. Learning to read between the lines and comprehend unspoken messages empowers us to better serve others and make more informed decisions in both personal and business interactions.

Exercise 19.1

Carefully scan the grid horizontally, vertically, and diagonally in all directions. Look for the words listed in the following key terms section. When you find a word, mark it to highlight its location. Words may be spelled forward or backward. Take your time and enjoy the challenge!

S	F	O	L	L	O	W	E	R	S	V	I	S	I
R	E	C	O	M	M	U	N	I	C	A	T	I	V
E	R	C	O	I	T	C	A	R	E	T	N	I	I
V	E	O	R	L	I	S	T	E	N	I	N	G	S
E	V	M	D	E	C	A	F	I	T	L	U	M	I
A	R	E	L	A	T	I	O	N	S	H	I	P	O
L	E	M	U	D	I	S	C	R	E	T	I	O	N
I	N	T	E	R	A	C	T	I	O	N	S	S	V
A	N	O	I	T	A	C	I	N	U	M	M	O	C

Words to Find

- *Vision*
- *Listening*
- *Relationship*
- *Discretion*
- *Communication*
- *Followers*
- *Interactions*
- *Secrets*
- *Reveal*
- *Multifaced*

Exercise 19.2 The Many Faces of You

Create a Faces of You chart with different roles or contexts in your life (e.g., spouse, friend, employee, leader, family member). Reflect on how you behave, communicate, and express yourself in each of these roles. Identify any areas where you adapt your "face" and note why you do so. Consider how this understanding can improve your relationships and leadership skills.

Exercise 19.3 The Leader's Burden

Think back to a time when you had to bear a significant burden for the sake of a family member, friend, or team. What emotions and challenges did you face at this time? What were the ultimate outcomes of this experience? Did this align with the concept of leadership and information control discussed in the chapter?

Share your thoughts in the provided space.

Activity 19.4 Attentive Listening Exercise

- When someone is talking to you through a medium, perhaps online or on the phone, take care not to multitask. Look at the person's face or pay complete attention to his or her voice.
- When speaking in person, notice body language and facial expression.
- Tune into both verbal and nonverbal clues. Frequently, what is not said is as important as what is said.

Write down your thoughts on the space provided:

Action Plan: Become a Stronger Communicator and Listener

1. Communication Adaptation: Adapt your communication style based on the situation and audience. Recognize when it's appropriate to share certain information and when it's best to keep certain aspects of your life private.
2. Leadership and Compassion: Embody the role of a leader who carries the burden of worry for the well-being of your team or loved ones. Protect them from unnecessary stress while still providing necessary guidance and support.

Remember!

Adapting your communication style is an ongoing process. Work on refining your leadership skills and being comfortable with your multifaceted self.

Summary and Encouragement

This chapter looks at the powerful concept of having multiple faces and the importance of keeping the larger picture in mind while making decisions and communicating. The Hebrew word *panim,* for face, is plural, reflecting the multifaceted nature of every individual. We learn that it is natural and proper to put on different faces for various situations, such as when dealing with family, colleagues, superiors, or friends.

This chapter also reviews the art of listening and reading between the lines to better understand others' thoughts and to make wiser business decisions. It explores the role of leaders in protecting their followers from unnecessary worries while maintaining a clear vision and command.

Secret #20

The Most Important Organ of Leadership Is Your Mouth

This chapter introduces a counterintuitive but crucial principle: the most important organ of leadership is your mouth. While the brain is undeniably vital, it is through effective communication that leaders truly shine. Whether you're a business professional, a doctor, a salesperson, or in any other profession that involves serving others, mastering the art of communication will significantly impact your success and income.

Consider the example of realtors—some struggle financially despite being in a potentially lucrative field. The key difference between successful real-estate professionals and those barely getting by often lies in how well they communicate and connect with their clients. Word of mouth, recommendations, and positive reviews are powerful factors that attract business. But how can you improve your communication skills and become a more effective speaker?

This workbook chapter is meant to help you follow through with the practical exercises and insights that were presented, helping you become a more eloquent speaker. It serves to reinforce the idea of listening to yourself speak, reading aloud, and developing your speaking skills in front of others. Pay attention to the valuable tips about making meaningful eye contact and using proper body language as you speak.

Learning to communicate effectively is a continuing process that requires dedication and practice. Unlock the full potential of your mouth as an essential business tool. Equip yourself with the skills to enhance your communication, elevate your career, and transform the way you connect with the world around you.

Let the power of your speech shape your future in ways you've never imagined. Your mouth is your instrument of influence—play it wisely and watch your life flourish!

Exercise 20.1

Unscramble the jumbled words after each statement to find the key concepts related to the chapter.

________________________**1.** The ability to convey ideas, thoughts, and emotions effectively using spoken words (MAINTOONCMUCI SILKSL)

________________________**2.** Recommendations and information spread through informal communication among individuals (ROWD FO HOTMU)

________________________**3.** The practice of fully concentrating, understanding, responding, and remembering what is being said during a conversation or speech (CAVITE TENNISLIG)

________________________**4.** Expressive movements of the hands, arms, or body used to emphasize or convey meaning during speech (SUREGETS)

________________________**5.** The act of delivering a speech or presentation to an audience, often in a formal setting (LIPCUB KINGSPEA)

Answers:

1. Communication skills; 2. Word of mouth; 3. Active listening; 4. Gestures; 5. Public speaking

Exercise 20.2 Reading Aloud Practice

Select a book, article, or speech that interests you and is suitable for reading aloud. Set aside 30 minutes three times a week for reading practice. Focus on enunciation, clarity, and fluency. You might choose to record yourself reading so that you can listen to yourself and identify areas for improvement. Make note of challenging words or phrases and practice them until you feel confident. In the following space, keep a list of your reading aloud material to help monitor your progress. List words that you want to incorporate into your speech.

Gradually increase the complexity and length of the material you read aloud.

Exercise 20.3 Word of Mouth Success Story

- Think about a specific instance where you received a positive referral or recommendation that had a significant impact on your life or career.
- Identify the qualities or skills that others appreciated in you, which resulted in the referral.
- Did effective communication play a role in creating a positive impression on those who referred you?
- Turn the noted experience into an anecdote that you can share at the dinner table or with a friend.
- Note any key takeaways and lessons learned.

Activity 20.4 Guided Reflection and Action Plan

- Reflect on your current communication abilities in different aspects of your life, including professional, social, and personal interactions. Consider areas where you excel and areas where you feel there is room for improvement.

- Contemplate the impact effective communication can have on your personal and professional life. Acknowledge that good communication skills are essential for building strong relationships, making a positive impression on others, and achieving success in your career.

- Be honest with yourself about any specific challenges you face in communication, such as public speaking anxiety, difficulty articulating ideas, or maintaining eye contact during conversations. Recognize that these challenges provide opportunities for growth.

- Recall instances in your life where effective communication resulted in positive outcomes, such as successful negotiations, gaining new clients, or resolving conflicts amicably. Recognizing these successes can boost your confidence and motivate you to improve further.

(*continued*)

Action Plan

1. Set Clear Communication Goals: Identify specific communication goals you want to achieve. For example: I will offer a comment or suggestion at our weekly business meeting. Make sure your goals are measurable.
2. Reading Aloud Practice: Commit to reading aloud as stated in the chapter. Focus on improving your enunciation, fluency, and overall speaking skills. Record yourself to track your progress.
3. Seek Opportunities for Public Speaking: Seek out opportunities to practice public speaking, whether it's at work meetings, social gatherings, or by joining a public speaking club like Toastmasters. Recognize each opportunity as a chance to refine your communication abilities and build confidence.
4. Practice Natural Gestures and Body Language: Experiment with using natural and expressive gestures during conversations and presentations. Observe how others use body language effectively and incorporate similar techniques into your own communication style.
5. Seek Constructive Feedback: Ask for feedback from trusted friends, family members, or mentors regarding your communication skills. Be open to constructive criticism and use it to refine your approach to communication.
6. Celebrate Your Progress: Recognize and celebrate your achievements along the way, no matter how small they may seem. Each step forward in improving your communication skills brings you closer to becoming a more effective communicator.
7. Stay Persistent and Patient: Improving communication is an ongoing journey that requires patience and persistence.

> **Remember!**
>
> Effective communication is a powerful tool that can boost your career prospects and enrich your personal relationships. By following this action plan and remaining committed to growth, you will unlock the potential of your most important organ—your mouth.

Summary and Encouragement

This chapter highlights the incredible power and significance of effective communication. While the brain is vital for processing information, it is through our mouths that we connect with others and convey our thoughts, ideas, and emotions. Just as realtors' successes depend on how well they communicate and connect with their clients, the success of most financial transactions hinges on the ability of the participants to effectively communicate with one another.

Good communication skills are not inherent talents but learned and honed abilities. Reading aloud to improve articulation and fluency and seeking opportunities to speak in public to build confidence are steps everyone can take. Natural gestures and body language enhance our message's impact, allowing us to connect on a deeper level with our audience.

Speaking is a skill that can be improved with practice and dedication. While fear of public speaking is widespread—or perhaps because of that fact—the rewards are immense. As you commit to refining your communication skills, you will see remarkable transformations in your personal and professional life.

Every interaction is an opportunity to hone your communication abilities. Embrace feedback and view each speaking engagement as a chance to grow. As you become more adept at articulating your thoughts and connecting with others, you will naturally inspire confidence and trust, qualities that are essential for business.

Never underestimate the power of your words and how they can positively impact those around you. By mastering the art of communication, you can influence, motivate, and uplift others, fostering strong relationships and achieving success in building your business.

Let your mouth become your most powerful tool for improving your income.

Secret #21

Recognizing What You Can't Do

You are now halfway finished with this book. We hope that you feel empowered and confident about the work you do and the money you earn. Secret #21 veers off on a slightly different path. Yes, you can do more and better than you imagine, but the chapter "Recognizing What You Can't Do" contains a warning: be wise in your choices.

As human beings touched by the Divine, few of us tap into our full capabilities. At the same time, swimming against the current is not always the wisest choice. We urge you to demand more from yourself, but not to expect to attain the unreachable. Perhaps these workbook exercises can help you to dream big while staying rooted in reality.

Exercise 21.1 Honest Self-assessment

Who doesn't love an inspiring story? Born without legs and given up for adoption by her birth parents, Jennifer Bricker's new family encouraged and supported her enjoyment of gymnastics, not letting her disability rule her life. Her accomplishments in that field are awe-inspiring. Only as a teenager did she discover that the woman most inspired her, Olympic gold medalist Dominique Moceanu, was actually her birth sister.

Let's unpack this story a bit. Clearly, there is an element of genetic talent here. There is also an indomitable spirit and an incredibly supportive family. Our challenge for you is to ask yourself whether your dreams should be pursued, just as Jennifer pursued hers, or whether you should redirect them in a way that you might have greater chance of accomplishing.

1. Do you have a big, audacious, bold dream?
2. How long has this been an aspiration of yours?
3. What steps have you taken to reach your goal?
4. How well do you handle disappointment?
5. Do you have reason to believe that you have specific gifts that make this goal reachable (genetics, support, family history, etc.)?
6. Are you willing to put in the time, effort, and sacrifice necessary to give this a shot?

My Conclusions

Exercise 21.2 Nature Versus Nurture: Knowing Yourself

Fill in the blanks or pick the most correct choice.

1. A disproportionate number of people in my family are ____________. (Examples: in the military, dentists, good with money, adventuresome)
2. A disproportionate number of people in my family are ____________. (Repeat this line as often as is useful.)
3. Growing up, I was (encouraged to) (discouraged from) experiment(ing) with different things and pursue(ing) many interests.
4. My tendency when I hit an obstacle is to (give up) (go around it) (plow straight ahead).
5. I believe that we are more the products of (nature) (nurture) (both equally)

My Thoughts

Activity 21.3 Plan B: Guided Reflection and Action Plan

If you have concluded that you are not driven to a superhuman extent or that you are more similar to 99% of people than you are to Jennifer Bricker or some of the other people mentioned in Secret #21, can you redirect your dreams in a more attainable direction?

- Reflect on what you would do to earn money in your wildest dreams.
- If that is not realistic, can you re-channel your desires in a practical way? For example: Perhaps you won't play a recital at Carnegie Hall, but you could build a business matching music teachers with students and facilitating the relationship by handling the business side of things.
- Consider whether you need to push yourself harder and demand more from yourself than you currently do.
- Pay attention to feedback from wise and good people who know you well and want you to succeed. A teacher of ours used to say, "If everyone around says that you are a duck, you should start quacking."

Action Plan

1. Set Priorities and Goals:
    - Mark dates in your calendar by which you should achieve certain steps toward your goals.
    - Seek a wise mentor who can help you honestly assess your strengths and weaknesses.
    - Look into variations on your dreams and research the options.

2. Work, Work, Work:
   - Throw yourself into reaching your goal.
   - Evaluate whether you are sincere in wanting to do what you think you want to do.
3. Reality Check:
   - Evaluate whether reaching for the mountain top instead of the moon may be the wisest choice.
   - Give your all to being happy with what you are doing.

Remember!

Keep two ideas in your mind simultaneously. As a human being you are capable of much more than you think. As a human being you have limitations.

Summary and Encouragement

We are rooting for you to accomplish more than you previously expected to accomplish. Be willing to work hard while also being willing to adjust to reality, based both on your past, including your family history as well as on your present "circumstances on the ground."

Secret #22

As Painful as Change Can Be, It Often Contains the Seeds of Growth

In this chapter, we discover the power of viewing change as an opportunity for transformation and success.

Change is an inevitable part of life. Whether we like it or not, we will all face moments of transition, upheaval, and uncertainty. At times, change may be sudden and overwhelming, leaving us feeling stressed and afraid.

This workbook chapter is designed to help you reflect on the ideas presented in Secret #22. Through guided reflection exercises and action plans, you will discover strategies to view change as a pathway to personal and professional growth.

Change can be painful, but it can also contain the seeds of growth and opportunity. It is our willingness to adapt, adjust, and remain true to our purpose that determines how we navigate through life's transitions.

You have the power to transform challenges into opportunities. Unlock the seeds of growth within you!

Exercise 22.1 Fill in the Blanks with Answers from Chapter 22

1. The biblical general in King David's army who understood the importance of fulfilling his purpose and serving God while being flexible in his approach: ____________________
2. The positive development or progress that change provides: ____________________
3. The inherent reason or objective that guides one's actions and decisions in life or business: ____________________
4. The way through which one acts to achieve one's purpose: ____________________
5. The creator and publisher of *TV Guide*: ____________________

Answers

1. Joab; 2. Opportunity; 3. Purpose; 4. Plans; 5. Walter Annenberg

Exercise 22.2 Purpose and Plan Alignment

It is easy to get committed to our plans without recognizing that reaching our true goals requires us to act in a different way. In our daily lives we may see this when we reach a detour in the road. If we insist that the only way to get to our lunch meeting is to drive down Elm Street, we will face frustration and give up if Elm Street is closed. If we recognize that Elm Street is the way we assumed was best to reach our luncheon appointment, but that is no longer true, then we can detour and take another route, still arriving at our goal.

How might you act differently if you keep your eye on the purpose (your goal) in the following situations rather than getting stuck on a specific plan?

1. You are running a service that cleans offices when offices are largely empty due to a huge shift to working from home.
2. You are a first-grade teacher when you discover that the reading method in which you were trained, and which you have used for the past five years, does not result in literacy and good reading skills.
3. You had vacation plans with a close friend, including airline tickets and reservations, when your friend cancels because of a family emergency.

Write down your thoughts in the following box.

Exercise 22.3

Identify any potential changes or adjustments you may need to make in your business life to stay aligned with your purpose while pursuing your goals.

1. What do you want to achieve professionally in the coming years?
2. Is there only one route to achieve certification or a degree in your area of interest?
3. Do you need to partner with someone to actualize your purpose?
4. Where does the path you are currently on lead?
5. Are there marked points along the path where you can stop and reassess?

Activity 22.4 Guided Reflection and Action Plan

Step 1: Reflect on Your Flexibility and Adaptability

1. Have you ever refused to accept the need for change?
2. Is there a specific change you have been avoiding but now realize could be an opportunity for growth?
3. Has staying in your comfort zone hindered your changing plans and moving in a new direction?

Step 2: Action Plan for Accepting Change

Based on your reflections, create an action plan for incorporating change into your life and aligning your goals with your purpose. Set specific and achievable steps that will help you navigate change effectively and stay true to your purpose.

Action Plan

1. Identify specific changes or adaptations needed to align your plans with your purpose.
2. Set realistic timelines for implementing these changes and monitor your progress.
3. Seek support from mentors, coaches, or friends who can provide guidance and encouragement.

Remember!

Change is a constant part of life that cannot be avoided. It can unlock new opportunities for personal and professional growth. Keep your eye on your purpose and be open to adaptation as you progress on your journey toward success and fulfillment.

Summary and Encouragement

Secret #22, "As Painful as Change Can Be, It Often Contains the Seeds of Growth," emphasizes the importance of adapting to change and aligning plans with your purpose. Change can be intimidating, but resisting it leads to stagnation. The chapter shares stories of individuals who were not crushed by unexpected obstacles in their lives, but rather overcame those hindrances and were energized by them to create new opportunities. It highlights the power of knowing what your end goal, your purpose is, and recognizing that the path to that goal may look different than you originally expected.

Develop the ability to navigate change while staying true to your purpose, and you will find that even amidst challenges, there lies the potential for growth and prosperity. Tackle change wholeheartedly, and you will discover fortune where you once saw only adversity.

Secret #23

Because Change Is a Constant Reality, Life Is More Accurately Depicted by a Video Than a Photograph

Welcome to the message encapsulated in Secret #23. In this chapter, we look at the notion that life is more similar to a video rather than a still photograph. Just like a video captures the passage of time and the unfolding of events, so does life constantly evolve, presenting us with new challenges and opportunities for growth.

Imagine you are shown two photographs, both depicting seemingly happy couples. At first glance, they might appear similar, but the truth lies beyond the snapshot. One couple enjoys a harmonious life together, dedicated to their family and future, while the other is entangled in a web of deceit, leading to eventual heartache and divorce. The photographs alone do not reveal the profound differences in their lives.

The analogy extends to our personal and professional pursuits. Too often, we focus on the present moment, failing to see the importance of considering the passage of time. Change is an inevitable part of life, and while it can be scary, it also brings forth tremendous opportunities for growth and success.

This workbook chapter will guide you in facing change with courage. With thought-provoking activities, guided reflections, and an action plan, we hope to help you navigate change with resilience and clarity. As you progress through these pages, remember that change is a constant reality, but with courage and strategic thinking, you can seize the opportunities that life presents.

Embody the notion of life as a video, where time unfolds before you, guiding you to the next chapter of your journey.

Exercise 23.1

Your mission is to navigate through the maze, following the sequence of letters that make up the title, from the letter B to the letter H, to find your way out.

1. Begin at the letter "B," indicated on the maze as the starting point.
2. Trace the path through the maze by following the sequence of letters in the title "Because Change Is a Constant Reality, Life Is More Accurately Depicted by a Video Than a Photograph."
3. Move through each letter in the exact order they appear in the title.
4. Continue tracing the path until you reach the letter "H" at the end of the title.

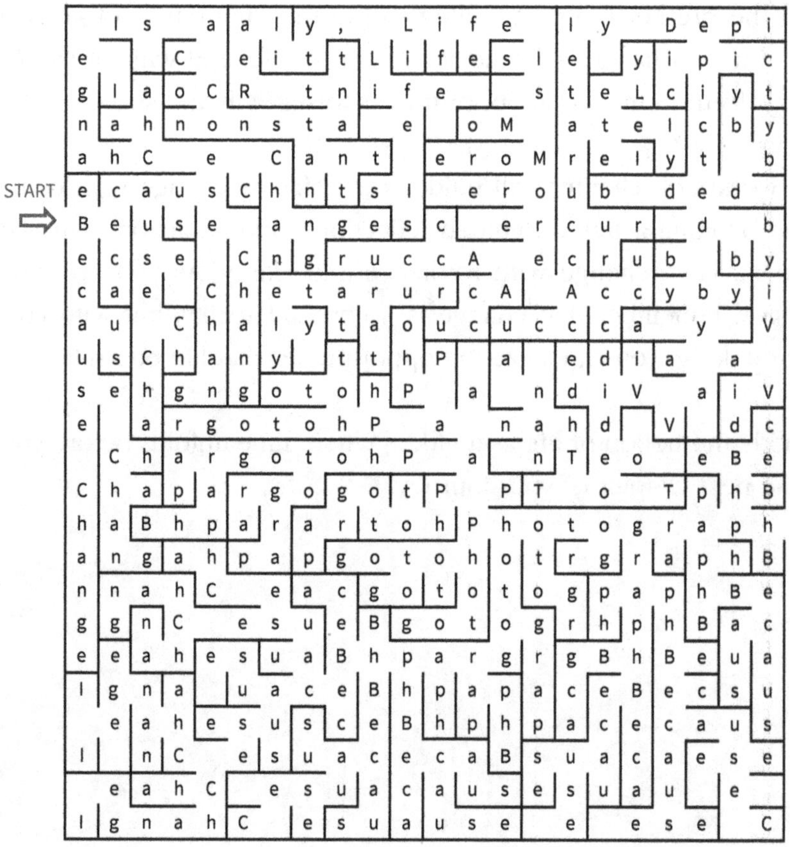

Solution

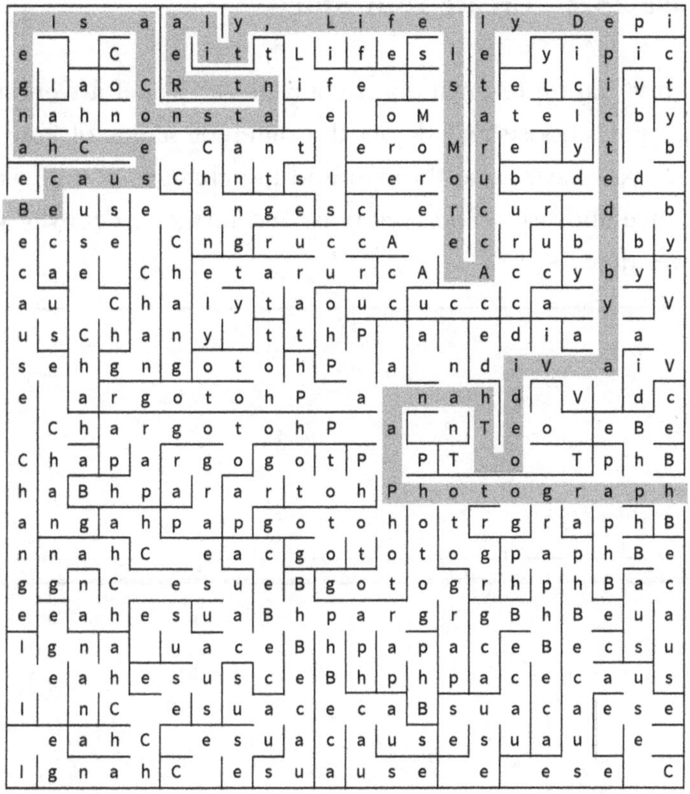

Exercise 23.2 Create Your Story

Write or draw a visual representation of your life story as if it were a video. Start from any point you choose and depict the different stages of your life, including the changes you have gone through and the changes you envision for your future. Be creative and use colors, symbols, and images to convey your journey and growth over time.

Exercise 23.3 Time Capsule of Change

Gather small items or pictures that represent important moments of change in your life. Get a container, such as a shoebox, and create a time capsule. You can decorate the outside of the box if you wish, making it personal and reflective of your journey. Place your chosen items inside. Write a short note about each item, explaining its significance and the change it represents. Store it in a safe place and put a tickler in your calendar for six months.

After six months, retrieve your time capsule and find a quiet space to open it privately. Reflect on your experience by answering the following questions:

- How did it feel to see the items and notes after six months?
- Did any memories or emotions surface as you opened the time capsule?
- Did your perception of the changes represented by the items change over the months?
- What insights or realizations did you gain from this exercise?

Keep your time capsule as a reminder of your growth and resilience. You might want to continue adding items to the capsule over time to document future moments of change.

Activity 23.4 Guided Reflection and Action Plan

1. Internalize the concept of change as a constant reality in life. Where you are today is a snapshot; you are interested in the video. Consider the examples of the two couples in the photographs and how their lives diverged over time due to the choices they made.
2. Consider your current mindset and attitude toward change. Are you open and adaptable to new circumstances, or do you tend to resist change out of fear or uncertainty?
3. Reflect on the role of courage in facing change. Recall the phrase *chazak v'ematz* from the Bible. Do you tend to have both the ability and the fortitude to deal with life's challenges, or is one or the other more difficult for you?
4. Envision the person you want to become and the accomplishments you wish to achieve in your personal and professional life.

Action Plan

1. Apply the video metaphor to your financial situation, business endeavors, or career path. Instead of focusing only on the current moment, evaluate your journey, anticipate future trends, and track your direction. Consider how a holistic view can guide your decision-making.
2. Acknowledge that change can be scary, even when it is for the better. Embrace the inevitability of change and recognize that courage is essential for navigating through it.
3. Utilize the three pathways outlined in the chapter for cultivating courage:
   - Analyze challenges separately: Break down complex problems into small, manageable steps.
   - Recognize the contagious nature of courage: Surround yourself with courageous individuals to boost your own courage.
   - Proactively seek strength in ancient Jewish wisdom: Be aware of needing to *chazak v'ematz* as you develop courage and willpower.

Remember!

When you see others who seem to be doing better than you, remember that you do not know the videos of their lives. You don't know the battles they fought or the mistakes they might be making today that will only be evident tomorrow. Focus on your own video.

Summary and Encouragement

"Because Change Is a Constant Reality, Life Is More Accurately Depicted by a Video Than a Photograph" reminds us that life is a continuous journey. Using the analogy of photographs versus videos, the chapter emphasizes that a single snapshot in time cannot capture the full complexity of life, which is better represented as a dynamic and evolving video.

The story of Miguel Rodriguez serves as an inspiring example of seizing opportunities. Miguel's life was challenging, but he remained positive, adaptable, and courageous. His willingness to face change head on led him to significant growth and success, elevating him to a higher position in his job and improving his family's quality of life.

Harness your skills, tools, and resources and combine them with the courage to act. Approach the future with determination. Life's challenges are not roadblocks but stepping stones, guiding us toward a more fulfilling and successful future.

The past influences the present, and the present influences our future. To help stay on that path, surround yourself with courageous individuals who will inspire and support you.

Secret #24

The More That Things Change, the More We Must Depend Upon Those Things That Never Change

Secret #24 of our workbook series explores the timeless wisdom of ancient Jewish teachings and its relevance in navigating the complexities of our ever-changing world. In this chapter, we delve into a principle that holds true through the ages: "The More That Things Change, the More We Must Depend on Those Things That Never Change."

Change is an inherent part of life, and in our modern world, it happens faster than ever before. We witness advancements in science, technology, and medicine reshaping the way we live and interact. From the invention of smartphones to the rise of artificial intelligence, the landscape of our existence is constantly evolving.

However, amidst this dynamic whirlwind of change, foundational truths remain steadfast and reliable. These enduring principles, rooted in God's blueprint, serve as our guiding lights amid uncertainty and disruption. They provide us with strength, wisdom, and courage as we face the challenges that come with progress and change.

We uncover how these unchanging principles offer timeless solutions to the dilemmas and uncertainties presented by progress. We learn that while technology may change, the core values of human interactions, spirituality, and ethics remain constant, guiding us through the complexities of the modern era.

Exercise 24.1

The first column contains a human need or desire. Use the second and third columns to fill in possible ways that this need or desire was met in the past and how it might be met currently. There are many correct answers. For example, we filled in the first line for you, but instead of "horse," we might have written "canoe"; instead of "airplane" we could have written "train."

Unchanging Need/Desire	Used to Be Filled By	Currently Filled By
Transportation	Horse	Airplane
Acquiring Food		
Education		
Companionship		
Meaning and Purpose in life		
Shelter		
Physical Health		
Spiritual Health		

Exercise 24.2 Robber Barons Versus Philanthropists

While everyone can and should behave charitably, it is a reality that the wealthier an individual is, the greater his or her donation can be.

Look around your city or one near you, do some research if necessary, and answer the following questions:

1. Are there hospitals or hospital wings and departments that were founded or funded by individuals rather than governments?
2. How much of your local library's funding for programming comes from the government and how much from nongovernmental gifts and grants?
3. Are there art centers, museums, or concert halls that were built by personal wealth?
4. Are you aware historically of the collapse of countries' economies that were caused by immoral and bad governmental choices?
5. Are you aware currently of the collapse of countries' economies that are being caused by immoral and bad governmental choices?

Jot down any thoughts you may have. Would your city be better off if it had no wealthy citizens, or conversely, is your city served by not having societal wealth?

Activity 24.3 Guided Reflection and Action Plan

We can rely on certain unchanging principles and truths to navigate the complexities of life. These principles, rooted in God's biblical blueprint, serve as pillars of strength, wisdom, and guidance in the face of change. Create an action plan for incorporating these unchanging principles into your life.

Step 1: Self-reflection on Change

- Think of the different areas of your life such as relationships, career, and personal growth. What tools do you use to manage these areas that were not available to a previous generation? Do you seek guidance from unchanging principles alongside using modern instruments?

Step 2: Identifying Unchanging Principles

- Recall the unchanging principles mentioned in the chapter, such as the concept of O-SH-R (wealth) as it pertains to society and the pillars of God, human nature, and the physical world. Consider how these principles play out in your life and how they can serve as a source of strength and guidance during times of change.

Step 3: Applying Unchanging Principles

How can you apply these unchanging principles in various aspects of your life? Consider the following examples.

- In your personal relationships, do you believe that character traits such as honesty, integrity, and commitment are or should be different today than they used to be?
- Do you believe that a society should limit the amount of wealth that a person can honestly accumulate? Is making sure that no individual earns substantially more than any other individual the best plan for a society?

Step 4: Developing an Action Plan

- Based on your reflections, create an action plan for integrating these unchanging principles into your life. Consider the following:
  - Set specific goals: Determine the areas of your life where you want to apply these unchanging principles and set achievable goals.

- Create reminders: Find ways to remind yourself of the chosen principles daily, such as writing them down, creating affirmations, or using symbolic objects.
- Seek guidance: Reach out to mentors, spiritual leaders, or individuals who embody these principles and learn from their experiences.

Step 5: Movement and Stability

- Cultivate a sense of humility that allows you to access the wisdom of the past.

Remember!

Use the strength of unchanging principles to guide your life journey. Be skeptical of new ideas when it comes to areas such as family or money. Draw from the wisdom of the past and unchanging truths to shape your path.

Summary and Encouragement

Profound wisdom is found in recognizing unchanging principles in the midst of a rapidly changing world. The chapter emphasizes the importance of acknowledging the dynamic nature of science, medicine, and technology, while also holding onto timeless truths. These unchanging principles act as pillars of strength, guiding individuals through the uncertainties and challenges of life. The concept of *O-SH-R* (wealth) is explored, demonstrating that wealth creation is essential for a thriving society and is governed by unchanging principles.

As you journey through life, remember that change is inevitable. The world around you will evolve in ways beyond your control, bringing both opportunities and disruptions. Recognize advancements in science and technology, but anchor yourself in unchanging principles that have stood the test of time.

In a world that can sometimes feel overwhelming and unpredictable, knowledge of God and an understanding of human nature, and the principles of the physical world remain constant. Take comfort in knowing that you have a solid foundation to build upon, regardless of external circumstances.

As you encounter change, challenge yourself to seek wisdom in ancient Jewish teachings and the unchanging truths they offer. Understand that wealth creation is not just about personal financial prosperity, but also about fostering a flourishing and morally upright society.

Your understanding of unchanging principles will enable you to face whatever comes your way. As you grow in your knowledge and application of these principles, you will find strength, wisdom, and courage to shape your life and impact the world around you positively.

May you be empowered to draw from the wellspring of unchanging truths as you navigate the ever-changing tides of life.

Secret #25

Press Forward Even When the Road Ahead Is Not Clear

Chapter 25 of our journey through the ancient Jewish wisdom empowers us to face the ever-changing world by pressing forward even when the road ahead seems uncertain or obscured.

In Deuteronomy, chapter 28, we find a profound verse that reveals the rewards and warnings promised to society at large that are tied to our adherence to unchanging principles. When we, as a society, choose to follow God's commandments, we unlock blessings such as prosperity, children, success, safety, and a life without want. However, if we neglect these principles and fail to serve with joy and jubilation, we will face hardships.

We must grasp the powerful lesson found in the story of Moses leading the Israelites out of Egypt. When faced with the seemingly insurmountable obstacle of the Red Sea, God instructed Moses to have the people march forward into the water. Only then did He part the waters. This powerful metaphor teaches us that to overcome challenges, we must act and move forward, trusting that the way will reveal itself in due course.

In business as in life, we will undoubtedly encounter trials and tribulations with no evident solution. The key to success lies not in endless contemplation but in doing. By exploring, testing hypotheses, and embracing trial and error, we pave the path forward.

However, understanding time is crucial in this process. Time is a complex dimension, and our perception of it can vary based on circumstances and experience. To fully appreciate change and navigate through it, we must learn to see things with fresh eyes, as if experiencing them for the first time, like Adam in the Garden of Eden.

The successful business professional understands that change is constant and continually looks ahead. Waiting for certainty or waiting for others to lead is a path to being left behind. Instead, take control of your destiny, make the most of every moment, and seek opportunities where others see uncertainty.

Exercise 25.1

Please read each question carefully and select the best answer from the choices provided. Each question has only one correct answer. Choose the option that you believe best aligns with the key concepts discussed in this chapter.

1. What lesson can we learn from the story of Moses leading the Israelites out of Egypt?

- **a.** Moses waited for the Red Sea to part before leading the people through.
- **b.** The Israelites crossed the Red Sea before it parted, demonstrating the need for action.
- **c.** Moses had a clear vision of the future before deciding to lead the Israelites out of Egypt.
- **d.** The Israelites were afraid and hesitant to enter the Red Sea.

2. How are problems best solved, according to the chapter's teachings?

- **a.** By taking action and moving forward, using trial and error
- **b.** By relying on others to provide solutions
- **c.** By sitting and thinking about them for an extended period
- **d.** By waiting for a clear and easy solution to present itself

3. What is the significance of time in our perception of the world?

- **a.** Time is straightforward and easy to understand.
- **b.** Time influences our perception of music and speech.
- **c.** Time has no impact on our lives.
- **d.** Time is only relevant in measuring length and weight.

4. Why is it crucial for business professionals to look ahead?

- **a.** Change is inevitable and must be avoided at all costs.
- **b.** Looking ahead creates unnecessary stress and anxiety.
- **c.** Looking ahead is not necessary as change is a rare occurrence.
- **d.** To be successful, one must anticipate future opportunities and challenges.

5. How should individuals approach the future when the road ahead is unclear?

a. Wait for others to pave the way before acting.

b. Approach the future with fear and hesitation.

c. Move forward with wisdom and courage.

d. Avoid the future and stick to the familiar.

Answer:

1. b; 2. a; 3. b; 4. d; 5. c

Exercise 25.2 Time and Perception

1. Review the section that discusses time and its impact on our perception of music and speech.
2. Set a timer for one minute and close your eyes. Focus on the passing of time without any external distractions.
3. After the minute is up, write down your thoughts and feelings about how time seemed to pass during this exercise.
4. Think about a joyful experience from your past. Share with a friend or relative how your perception of time during that experience differed from the one-minute exercise.
5. Consider how understanding the complexity of time can help you appreciate how time is relative and subjective.

Activity 25.3 Future-forward Thinking in Business

1. Research and identify one emerging trend or technology relevant to your field of work or industry.
2. Write a few sentences exploring the potential impact of this trend on your industry and how it may shape the future of your profession.
3. Brainstorm three innovative ideas or strategies that could help you adapt to this trend and leverage it to your advantage.
4. What are possible negative consequences or pitfalls of this technology and/or being an early adopter?
5. Discuss your ideas with a colleague or mentor, seeking feedback and additional insights.
6. Create a personal action plan outlining how you will implement one of your innovative ideas to stay ahead in your professional journey.

Activity 25.4 Guided Reflection and Action Plan

In this chapter, we examined the story of Moses and the Israelites crossing the Red Sea, which taught us the valuable lesson of moving firmly forward even when the path ahead is not clear. Additionally, we recognized how the concept of time impacts our perception of the world, emphasizing the need to appreciate time and use it wisely to stay ahead in an ever-changing world.

Take some time to reflect on the key concepts from this chapter and how they resonate with your own experiences and beliefs.

1. Learning from the Story of Moses: Consider a significant challenge you faced in the past. Did you approach it with courage and faith, like

(*continued*)

Moses and the Israelites crossing the Red Sea, or did you hesitate and wait for certainty? Reflect on the lessons you can draw from that experience and how they should inform your future actions when facing uncertainty.

2. Problem-solving with action: Recall a problem you recently encountered. How did you approach finding a solution? Did you spend excessive time contemplating the problem? Think about how your approach affected the outcome and how you can incorporate the principle of taking action before all the facts are in.
3. Time and Perception: Explore how your perception of time influences your daily life. Do you often feel rushed or like time is slipping away? Consider how understanding the complexities of time can help you appreciate the present moment.

Action Plan

Based on your reflections, create a personalized action plan to implement the key concepts from this chapter into your life.

1. Move Forward: Identify one area of your life where you tend to hesitate. Develop a mindset of openness and willingness to adapt to new circumstances. Seek opportunities to consider how acting with more alacrity can lead to personal growth and new possibilities.
2. Practice Faithful Action: Choose one upcoming challenge or project in your professional life. Instead of waiting for certainty, commit to taking proactive steps toward a solution. Trust in your abilities and the process and be willing to adjust your approach if needed.
3. Time Management and Appreciation: Set aside specific moments each day for time organization. Use this time to appreciate the present, acknowledge your accomplishments, and plan for the future. Practice being fully present in your daily activities and interactions without constantly feeling rushed.
4. Future-forward Thinking: Stay informed about emerging trends and advancements in your industry. Regularly seek out opportunities for

professional development and skill enhancement to stay ahead of the curve. See the opportunities for growth and actively seek ways to innovate and adapt in your field.

Remember!

Press forward even when the road ahead is not clear. Make time your ally as you travel on a journey of continuous growth and success.

Summary and Encouragement

This chapter teaches that despite the unpredictability of tomorrow, we should face it with confidence and courage. The teachings from Deuteronomy reminded us of the rewards and consequences that come with our choices, emphasizing the importance of following unchanging principles to guide our actions. The story of Moses and the Israelites crossing the Red Sea exemplifies the invaluable lesson of moving forward, even when the path ahead is not clear. Understanding the complexities of time allowed us to appreciate the present moment and perceive change as an opportunity for growth and innovation.

Trust in your abilities to navigate the unknown. Like the Israelites who marched into the water before the sea parted, be bold and take a leap of faith. Keep an open mind and a positive attitude as you encounter challenges, for it is through acting that solutions are found.

Time, with its mysterious ways, is both your ally and a reminder to appreciate the beauty of each moment. Make the most of your time, be fully present in your pursuits, and remain receptive to change. The world is ever-evolving, and by staying proactive and future-forward, you can position yourself for success in an ever-changing landscape.

Secret #26

Do Not Let Fear Conquer You—Press On

Fear is a natural emotion that can be daunting, but it's an integral part of growth and achieving our goals. We demonstrate how to navigate fearful moments through stories from the Bible as well as more modern examples.

At times, stepping into the unknown can be terrifying, but it is essential for our personal and professional development. Eliminating fear is not the answer; rather, we must learn to cope with it. Just as Moses and the Israelites had to walk into the water before it split, we too must face our fears head-on and press forward.

We studied the example of Malcolm McLean, who revolutionized the shipping industry with his standardized freight container, despite causing major changes and fears among dockworkers. Change is inevitable, and learning to deal with it is a key to our growth and success.

Drawing parallels between the lives of Joseph and Judah from the book of Genesis, we explored the idea that making mistakes is part of being human as is being mistreated. Mistakes or the pain that can come through trusting and working with others, though daunting, should not be feared, as they are stepping stones to wisdom and growth. We must be clear that no one achieves greatness without encountering missteps and injuries along the way.

In the workbook exercises, you'll have the opportunity to reflect on your own experiences with fear, change, and facing mistakes. Through self-reflection and guided activities, you'll gain insights into how to build courage and resilience in the face of fear. This chapter is not about eliminating fear entirely, which is a quixotic quest. It is about harnessing its power and using it to propel ourselves forward.

Exercise 26.1

Test your understanding of the key concepts from the chapter. Fill in the blanks with the correct answer for each question.

1. Facing fear and pressing forward is essential for success in business and ________.
2. ________ is an emotion that is a natural part of encountering unknown and challenging situations.
3. Overcoming fear is not about eliminating it, but rather about learning to ________ with it.
4. ________ wrote the book of Ecclesiastes, in which he recognized that being a person of action and accomplishment invariably means sometimes taking wrong steps.
5. ________ is the innovative man who transformed the shipping industry with his standardized freight container, despite the disruption his invention would cause.
6. Making mistakes is an inherent part of being human, and it is vital to accept them as opportunities for growth and ________.
7. In the book of Genesis, ________'s life is explored in parallel with Joseph's, highlighting the theme of overcoming both mistakes and ill treatment.

Answers:

1. life; 2. Fear; 3. cope; 4. King Solomon; 5. Malcolm McLean; 6. wisdom; 7. Judah

Exercise 26.2 Fear Exploration

- Write down specific instances or situations where you felt fearful and how you reacted to those situations.
- Write about your feelings, thoughts, and the impact of fear on your decision-making.
- Write down your insights and experiences.

Exercise 26.3 Learning from Mistakes

Read the story of "Harmony Farms: Turning Setbacks into Success."

Story of Harmony Farms

Harmony Farms is a small, family-owned organic farm that started with a dream of providing fresh, healthy produce to its local community. The founders, Sarah and Tom, were passionate about sustainable farming practices and believed in the importance of organic food.

In the beginning, things seemed promising, and the farm gained a small but dedicated customer base. However, as the business expanded, they faced several challenges and made some costly mistakes. One year, a sudden storm destroyed a significant portion of their crops, leading to financial strain. In another instance, they invested heavily in a new irrigation system that turned out to be faulty and wasted precious resources.

Amidst these setbacks, Sarah and Tom felt discouraged and questioned their ability to continue. But instead of giving up, they decided to view these mistakes as opportunities for growth. They sought advice from experienced farmers, attended workshops on sustainable agriculture, and learned from their missteps.

One crucial lesson they took from these challenges was the need to diversify their crops and income streams. They started offering farm tours, hosting workshops on organic gardening, and selling value-added products like homemade preserves and organic soaps. These initiatives not only brought in additional revenue but also strengthened their connection with the local community.

With determination and perseverance, Harmony Farms managed to turn its setbacks into successes. Sarah and Tom became known for their commitment to sustainable practices, and their products gained popularity in nearby cities. Despite the initial hardships, they built a thriving business that not only sustained their family but also contributed to the well-being of their community.

Analyze the story, identify the mistakes made by Sarah and Tom, and discuss how these mistakes contributed to the farm's ultimate success. Write down your findings and key takeaways from the story.

Activity 26.4 Guided Reflection and Action Plan

In this chapter, we explored the significance of facing fear, taking courageous action, and learning from mistakes and negative experiences as crucial components of personal and professional growth. Review the concepts discussed so that you can gain insights into your own fears, the impact of fear on your decisions, and how to develop strategies for overcoming obstacles.

1. Self-Reflection on Fear: Take a moment to identify your most significant current fears in both your personal and professional life. Consider how these fears are influencing your decisions and actions. Ask yourself the following questions:
   - What are the specific fears that are holding me back from pursuing my goals?
   - How are these fears affecting my progress in both business and life?
   - Is fear preventing me from taking necessary actions?
   - What is the worst possible outcome if I act and discover that I made a mistake?
   - How likely is the worst possible outcome to occur?

2. Acknowledging Mistakes: Consider the following questions.
   - What are some significant mistakes I've made?
   - Did these mistakes lead to any personal or professional development?
   - Was I able to move forward from these mistakes?
   - Am I open to viewing mistakes as opportunities for growth and improvement?

3. Recognizing Courageous Actions:
    - When have I shown courage and determination in my personal or professional life?
    - What motivated me to take those courageous actions?
    - How did these actions contribute to positive outcomes or personal growth?

Action Plan

1. Set Courageous Goals:
    - Identify at least one ambitious goal in your personal and professional life that may require facing fear and uncertainty.

      Example:
    - Personal Goal: Improve public speaking skills by participating in a local community speaking event.
    - Professional Goal: Initiate a new project at work that involves collaborating with colleagues from different departments.
2. Plan for Fear Management:
    - Create a fear management plan for each of your courageous goals. Outline specific strategies to cope with fear and uncertainty when working toward these objectives.

Example:

- Practice public speaking in front of a supportive group of friends or family to build confidence.
- Break down the new project into smaller tasks, setting achievable milestones to track progress.

3. View Mistakes as Learning Opportunities:

- Shift your perspective on mistakes and setbacks. Instead of avoiding failure, acknowledge that everyone fails at times.

Example:

- If you face challenges during the speaking event, assess what went wrong, seek feedback, and work on improving weaknesses for future speeches.
- If you encounter obstacles in the new project, collaborate with team members to brainstorm solutions and adjust the plan accordingly.

4. Celebrate Progress and Resilience:

- Acknowledge your achievements, no matter how small, and celebrate your progress. Recognize the courage and resilience you demonstrate throughout your journey.

Remember!

Face the challenges ahead, view mistakes as opportunities, and take courageous steps toward your goals. With your fear management plan and a support system in place, you'll discover new heights of personal and professional development. Courage does not eliminate fear; it empowers you to press on despite it.

Summary and Encouragement

Secret #26, "Do Not Let Your Fear Conquer You—Press On," explores the significance of facing fear, taking courageous actions, and learning from mistakes on the path to success in both business and life. Fear is a natural emotion that can hold us back, but instead of thinking that we can eliminate fear, we must learn to cope with it and forge ahead despite its presence. Like climber Alex Honnold, we can turn fear into a friend.

Just like the successful story of Harmony Farms, setbacks and missteps can lead to resilience, new strategies, and ultimately, success. As you journey forward, remember that fear is a normal part of the process. It is a sign that you are not staying stationary. The key is to develop a fear management plan and take action despite uncertainty.

View mistakes not as failures but as valuable lessons that help you refine your approach and grow stronger. When reversals are due to no fault of your own, be willing to try again despite your disappointment. No one achieves greatness without encountering obstacles and setbacks.

Secret #27

Become Strongly, Even Radically, Open to New Directions, Soft Sounds, and Faint Footsteps

Imagine sitting at your kitchen table late at night, the house quiet and still as you concentrate on your work. During these serene moments, you notice the soft hum of the refrigerator, a sound that goes unnoticed during the hustle and bustle of the day. This experience teaches us a powerful lesson: when everything around us is loud and chaotic, we often miss the subtle cues and faint footsteps of approaching opportunities.

This chapter encourages us to create moments of stillness and openness in our lives. Discover the concept of being in a receptive mode, blocking out distractions, and allowing thoughts to flow freely. By taking a few secluded moments on a regular basis, we can cultivate a receptive mindset that can lead to creative breakthroughs and innovative ideas.

By challenging ourselves to leave behind the familiar and be open to new directions, we can move forward in both our personal and professional lives.

Let us begin this journey together, becoming strongly, even radically, open to new directions, soft sounds, and faint footsteps.

Exercise 27.1

1. What is the primary reason the author enjoys working at the kitchen table at night?

   a. The kitchen table is more comfortable.

   b. The kitchen is quiet but still holds the feel of his family.

   c. The author can enjoy a midnight snack while working.

   d. The family is more attentive in the kitchen at night.

2. Why is it easier to hear the refrigerator running at night compared to during the day?

   a. The refrigerator is louder at night.

   b. The author's hearing is better at night.

   c. Daytime noise drowns out the refrigerator's sound.

   d. The refrigerator only runs at night.

3. What does the author suggest regarding spending time alone in a quiet place?

   a. It's unnecessary and a waste of time.

   b. It should be done every day for at least an hour.

   c. It's beneficial and should be scheduled regularly.

   d. It's impossible in today's busy world.

4. What does the Sabbath encourage?

   a. Catching up on chores

   b. Putting in extra hours at the office

   c. Fasting

   d. Being in a receptive mode

5. How does the chapter illustrate the importance of changing direction?

a. Through the example of William Wrigley

b. By emphasizing the need to stick to one's original plan

c. By showing that change is often unsuccessful

d. By accepting our nature

Answers:

1. b; 2. c; 3. c; 4. d; 5. a

Exercise 27.2 Weekly Moments of Stillness

- Set aside 10 to 15 minutes when you can be entirely alone and undisturbed.
- Find a quiet and comfortable space where you can sit and reflect without distractions.
- Dim the lights to reduce visual stimuli and create a calming atmosphere.
- During this time, let your thoughts flow freely without judgment or pressure.
- Practice being open and receptive to any insights or inspirations that come to you during this period.
- After the session, take a few moments to jot down any significant thoughts or ideas that emerged during your time of stillness.
- Make this a weekly ritual to enhance your ability to listen to your inner voice.

Exercise 27.3 Change Your Perspective Exercise

- Choose a regular activity or task that you perform, such as cooking a meal, driving to work, or completing a work assignment.
- Challenge yourself to change your perspective on the task. For example, if it's cooking a meal, experiment with new ingredients or cooking techniques.
- Perform the activity in this new way and notice any differences in your experience and outcomes.
- Reflect on the exercise and note any insights or ideas that emerged from the process of changing your routine.
- Repeat this exercise with different activities to strengthen your ability to be open to new directions and approaches.

Activity 27.4 Guided Reflection and Action Plan

In this chapter, we explored the importance of cultivating moments of silence and receptivity and being open to new directions in both our personal and professional lives. This chapter also presents a powerful message about the significance of leaving behind the old and overcoming fear and complacency. This reflection and action plan will help you integrate these principles into your life.

Guided Reflection

1. Think about a recent instance in your life where you ignored red flags that, in retrospect, were there for you to see. What techniques did you use in order not to pay attention to these warning signs? What might have happened if you had been more willing to focus on what was wrong?
2. How often do you find yourself in a quiet place, free from any pulls on you? Do you utilize these moments to sit quietly, or do you grab for your phone or utilize another distraction? Are you comfortable doing nothing?
3. Do you carry baggage from your past that stops you from living in the present and moving forward? Are you able to leave things behind, or does your mind frequently rehash older memories?
4. What major pivots have you made in your life? These might include changing the focus of your studies or business or moving to a new city or country. Do you acclimate relatively quickly to new circumstances, or does it take you a long time to develop your equilibrium anew?

Action Plan

1. Implement Exercise 27.2: Weekly Moments of Stillness. During this time, disconnect from electronic devices and let your thoughts flow without distractions.
2. Identify one area of your life, whether it's your career, a personal project, or a relationship, where you feel change is needed. Exploring a

new direction in that area. It could be as simple as researching or listening to a podcast on the topic.

3. Challenge yourself to think outside the box. If your employment/business ended tomorrow and you needed to find a new path, what might it be?
4. Gather your work team or social or family group and discuss whether maintaining the status quo in all areas is the best strategy. Is there a new direction that is worth exploring, even if it is as simple as changing the day of the week on which weekly meetings are held?
5. Don't make changes for the sake of making changes, but don't wait for a crisis to think of new directions.

Remember!

Tap into your inner wisdom and intuition to unlock a path to personal and professional growth. Give yourself the opportunity to hear faint footsteps that can lead you toward a bright future.

Summary and Encouragement

Secret #27, "Become Strongly, Even Radically, Open to New Directions, Soft Sounds, and Faint Footsteps," emphasizes the importance of being open and receptive to new ideas and directions. Several real-life examples illustrate the power of pivoting and listening to instincts when faced with challenges.

The chapter highlights the significance of setting aside dedicated time for oneself in a quiet space, free from distractions, and encourages readers to be open to the possibility that your intuitive inner voice is trying to tell you something important. Stillness provides individuals with the opportunity to hear murmurings that are easily drowned out during our busy days.

Sit in quiet reflection on a regular basis. Prioritize taking the time to get away from the clutter of daily life.

Don't be shackled to preconceived notions. Be willing to pivot when necessary. Just like great companies and successful individuals who charted new courses, you too can step away from the familiar and venture into unexpected territory.

Believe in the whisper of inspiration that guides you. It may be soft, but it might carry the power to transform your life. As you cultivate receptivity, watch how the barely discernible whispers of approaching opportunities become clearer and lead you toward your destiny.

Secret #28

Use the Power of Words, Sentences, and Sound

Secret #28 emphasizes the profound significance of language and the power it holds in shaping our lives, relationships, and success. Just as the exodus of the Israelites from Egypt symbolizes a journey from darkness to light, from pessimism to promise, this chapter explores how we can harness the power of words, sentences, and sound to bring about positive transformations in our own lives.

As we review ancient Hebrew wisdom passed down through generations, we discover that the Hebrew word *Pesach* not only translates to "Pass over," but also means "talking mouth." It alludes to the need for communication, conversation, and questions in order for there to be freedom. Questions are irresistible forces that initiate dialogue and lead to growth, both in personal and professional relationships.

The Hebrew word for desert, *midbar*, symbolizing an empty and solitary place, also bears the meaning of "speaking." This connection between the desert and communication reveals the importance of using our mouths to free ourselves from internal deserts—places of solitude and emptiness. By engaging in meaningful conversations, we effect a profound impact on our relationships, performance, and overall well-being.

The chapter emphasizes the significance of spoken language over text or digital communication. Face-to-face conversations foster deeper connections and enhance understanding, essential in both personal and professional dealings.

By appreciating the true potency of words, sentences, and sound in shaping your destiny, you acquire the tools to create more focused and productive days, foster stronger relationships, and stride toward your goals.

Are you ready to unlock the true power of language and become a master of communication? Journey toward your own "Promised Land" with the power of words.

Exercise 28.1

Unscramble the jumbled words after each statement to find the key terms related to the chapter.

____________________ **1.** A Hebrew word with a dual meaning. It translates to "Passover" but also signifies "talking mouth." (SPEACH)

____________________ **2.** The Hebrew word for desert, which carries not only the meaning of an empty place but also "speaking." (BIDRAM)

____________________ **3.** A powerful tool for initiating conversation and interaction. (STONESUIQ)

____________________ **4.** The process of breaking down significant goals into manageable, actionable tasks. (MALLS PESTS)

____________________ **5.** A wise salesperson knows not only the power of speech, but also the power of this. (CEESLIN)

Answers:

1. *Pesach*; 2. *Midbar;* 3. Questions; 4. Small steps; 5. Silence

Exercise 28.2 Conversation Starter Cards

- Create a set of Conversation Starter Cards. Write down 10 open-ended questions on separate index cards. These questions should encourage discussion and promote deeper connection.
- Carry these cards with you or keep them accessible to use in various situations, such as social gatherings, meetings, or family dinners.
- Challenge yourself to initiate conversations with others using the Conversation Starter Cards. Be an active listener and encourage the other person to share their thoughts and feelings.
- Note any insights gained through these conversations.

Exercise 28.3 "Talk Show Host" Reflection

- Imagine you are a talk show host for a popular TV show.
- Create a character for yourself as the host, complete with a name and persona.
- Record a mock interview with yourself as the host, discussing the key concepts of the chapter as if you were interviewing an expert on communication.
- During the interview, highlight your own insights and experiences related to communication, using the key terms and concepts from the chapter.
- After the recording, listen to or watch the interview and observe your communication style, gestures, and overall performance.
- What are your strengths and areas for improvement as a "talk show host" and communicator?

Activity 28.4 Guided Reflection and Action Plan

Consider the key concepts from the chapter.

1. The Power of Words: Consider the impact that words have on your life. How do the words you use influence your thoughts and emotions? How do they affect your interactions with others? Think about instances when the right words brought about positive change or when the wrong words led to misunderstandings.
2. The Importance of Communication: Reflect on the significance of communication in both personal and professional aspects of your life. How has effective communication played a role in your success and relationships? Have there been times when communication breakdowns led to challenges or missed opportunities?
3. The Art of Asking Questions: Do you utilize questions in initiating conversations and fostering understanding? Have you experienced the power of asking thought-provoking questions in various situations? How can you improve your questioning skills to engage others and build stronger connections?
4. Harnessing the Power of Speech: Think about the influence of your spoken words on your mindset and actions. Have you experienced situations when speaking aloud helped you gain clarity and motivation? How can you utilize the power of speech to bring positive changes in your life?
5. The Impact of Language on Planning: Reflect on how language and written communication help in planning and organizing your goals. How can you use sentences and paragraphs to structure your ideas and tasks effectively? Have you noticed improvements in productivity and focus when you write down your plans?

(*continued*)

Action Plan

Now that you have reflected on the key concepts, let's create an action plan to apply these insights in your daily life:

1. Mindful Word Choices: Pay close attention to the words you use in your interactions with others and in your self-talk. Choose words that uplift, inspire, and encourage. Avoid negative or harmful language. Practice mindful communication to promote positive relationships.
2. Strengthening Communication Skills: Dedicate time each day to practice effective communication. Engage in meaningful conversations with family, friends, colleagues, or even strangers. Focus on understanding their perspectives and responding thoughtfully.
3. Deploy the Power of Questions: Make it a habit to ask more questions in your conversations. Use open-ended questions that encourage deeper discussions and build stronger connections with others. Seek to learn from every interaction.
4. Speak Aloud for Clarity: When faced with important decisions or challenges, take the time to speak your thoughts and feelings aloud. Verbalizing your concerns and aspirations can provide clarity and help you identify the best course of action.
5. Writing for Organization and Focus: Use writing as a tool to organize your plans, goals, and daily tasks. Write full sentences and paragraphs to create a clear narrative for yourself. Maintain a journal, planner, or digital notes to keep track of your progress and stay focused on your objectives.

Remember!

With consistent practice, you'll experience the transformative power of words, sentences, and sound in shaping a brighter and more fulfilling future.

Summary and Encouragement

Secret #28, "Use the Power of Words, Sentences, and Sound," explores the profound impact of language and communication in our lives. Drawing from the exodus of the Israelites from Egypt, the chapter emphasizes the significance of speaking and asking questions as catalysts for transformation and deliverance. Through various examples and insights, the authors highlight how words and sentences shape our thoughts, relationships, and actions, ultimately influencing every aspect of our lives.

Your ability to communicate effectively is a superpower that can open doors, solve problems, and uplift those around you. Use your words with intention, for they have the power to improve not only your life but also the lives of others. As you harness the energy of speech and communication, you become a catalyst for growth and positive change, both in your personal journey and in the world around you.

Secret #29

Feeling Right About Money Makes You Act Right

We are moving right along and have reached Chapter 29 of our workbook! This chapter examines a crucial aspect of success in both business and life: our relationship with money. The analogy of self-defense emphasizes the importance of acting instinctively and instantaneously, but how does that relate to our approach to money? Feeling right about money is the key to acting right when it comes to financial decisions and opportunities.

Having technical financial knowledge isn't enough if you don't feel right about money deep within your soul. We cannot ignore that our feelings influence our thoughts, actions, and ultimately, our success in business and wealth creation.

Modern society often perpetuates negative associations with wealth, leading many to feel uncomfortable or ashamed when dealing with money. These negative feelings can hinder our success in business and prevent us from realizing our true potential.

Setting aside all preconceived notions about money and wealth is helpful in gaining an accurate perspective on money, which relatively few people appreciate. Adjusting your feelings about money will pave the way for acting right, and together, they will unlock the doors to a prosperous and fulfilling future.

Exercise 29.1

Determine whether each statement is True or False based on the key concept discussed in this chapter. Write "True" if the statement aligns with the chapter's message and write "False" if it does not.

____________________ **1.** Feeling right about money is solely a matter of positive thinking and intellectual understanding.

____________________ **2.** Money and blood share similarities in that they are both uncountable nouns and fungible.

____________________ **3.** Developing the right business spirit is essential for success in business.

____________________ **4.** Acting instinctively and appropriately with money is possible only through extensive analysis and calculation.

____________________ **5.** Feeling right about money means believing that wealth is a product of greed and selfishness.

____________________ **6.** Internalizing the right way to feel about money requires repetition and practice over time.

____________________ **7.** Our feelings have no impact on our physiological state or decision-making processes.

____________________ **8.** Money is considered a lifeblood because it is essential to all aspects of our lives.

____________________ **9.** Money is not a vital economic marker of wealth and has little significance in business.

____________________ **10.** Feeling correctly about money increases the likelihood of your making effective business decisions.

Answers:

1. False; 2. True; 3. True; 4. False; 5. False; 6. True; 7. False; 8. True; 9. False; 10. True

Exercise 29.2 Mindful Money Moments

1. Pick a 90-minute span of time when you are working or shopping to focus on "Mindful Money Moments."
2. Throughout that time, be aware of any thoughts related to the decisions you are making or the actions you are taking.
3. Ask yourself the following questions:
   a. How do I feel about this financial decision or transaction?
   b. Am I acting out of a negative mindset, or am I feeling confident and positive about my choices?
   c. Is this decision aligned with my beliefs about money being a product of value creation and service?
4. Jot down your mindful money moments in the space provided.

Exercise 29.3 Exploring Money Metaphors

1. Read the section of the chapter that discusses money as a lifeblood and its connection to other concepts.
2. Reflect on connections you can draw between money and various aspects of life, such as the following:
   - **a.** Money as a motivator to bring about positive change in your life
   - **b.** Money as a reflection of one's values and priorities
   - **c.** Money as a resource for personal growth and learning
3. Write down your realizations in the space provided.

Activity 29.4 Guided Reflection and Action Plan

1. How do you currently feel about money? Do you present the price for your services or your salary requests with confidence? Bravado? Diffidence?
2. Do you appreciate the value of your time and effort?
3. Consider the impact of your feelings about money on your business decisions and actions. Have there been instances where your feelings about money affected your behavior or choices in business?
4. Do you think of money as essential to all aspects of your life or are you annoyed that money factors into your decisions and what you can and cannot do?

Action Plan

Create an action plan to develop a positive and constructive relationship with money.

1. Identify any beliefs or feelings about money that you want to change. Write them down and challenge them with rational and positive counterarguments.
2. Engage in self-education about money and wealth. Read books, listen to podcasts, or attend seminars that promote a positive and healthy understanding of money. Learn about successful individuals who have created wealth through service and value creation.
3. Practice gratitude for money and the opportunities it provides. Each day, take a moment to express gratitude for the money you have and the opportunities it brings to take care of your family's needs and provide for your life.

(continued)

4. Surround yourself with like-minded individuals who also value money as a tool for positive impact. Engage in discussions with friends or colleagues who share a healthy perspective on money and business.
5. Monitor your thoughts and feelings about money regularly. If you notice any negative beliefs resurfacing, consciously redirect your thinking toward positive and constructive perspectives.

Remember!

You can develop a healthy and empowering relationship with money that will positively influence your actions and decisions in business and life. Feeling right about money allows you to act right and opens the door to greater success and fulfillment in your professional endeavors.

Summary and Encouragement

This chapter discusses the importance of developing a positive and constructive relationship with money. Drawing parallels to self-defense, the chapter emphasizes that instinctive action in any situation, including financial decisions, is only possible when there is a seamless unity between body, soul, and mind. The key is to internalize the knowledge of money, moving it from the head to the heart, so that actions are guided by intuitive and positive feelings.

Money is an economic lifeblood, essential to all aspects of life and business. The chapter encourages readers to recognize that feeling right about money is fundamental to acting as a successful business professional.

Stay committed to educating yourself about money and surrounding yourself with like-minded individuals. As you align your thoughts, feelings, and actions with the understanding that money is a tool for good, you will find yourself making wiser financial decisions and achieving greater success in your business endeavors.

Secret #30

You Can Best Attract What You Best Understand

Understanding something is crucial when seeking to attract it into our lives. This principle applies not only to money but to all aspects of our endeavors. To illustrate this point, we look at the example of salmon fishing. We also see how money comes into existence with the help of the story of Grandpa Lapin.

Throughout the workbook, you will find exercises, reflections, and practical examples to help you internalize these concepts. This workbook should help you have a deeper understanding of money's role in your life and how you can leverage this knowledge to attract greater prosperity and success.

Exercise 30.1

Match the key terms and key concepts from Secret #30 with their corresponding descriptions:

1. What is left over after deducting the costs of a business transaction

2. An individual who engages in trading, buying, and selling items for a profit

3. The state of having an abundance of valuable possessions or resources

4. Anything that is generally accepted as a medium of exchange, a measure of value, and a store of wealth

5. The online version of Grandpa Lapin

A. Money

B. Profit

C. eBay

D. Wealth

E. Business professional

Answers:

1. B; 2. E; 3. D; 4. A; 5

Exercise 30.2 The Power of the Peddler

The story of Grandpa Lapin illustrates how money is made—not redistributed. We can all "grow the pie" by facilitating transactions between individuals that leave both sides happier. Unfortunately, many people feel guilty when they make money by buying something from one place and selling it at a profit.

Let's look at a few examples of this. Based on what you have learned from this book so far, gauge your reaction to each circumstance.

1. The Student Government Organization (SGO) arranges to buy bulk supplies of chocolate bars. Each bar costs them $1.25. The SGO sells the bars in the student store for $1.50 apiece.
   a. Should this be forbidden because the SGO is making a profit?
   b. Should this be forbidden because the SGO is making an unreasonable profit?
   c. Should it be allowed because the SGO is going to use the profits to hold an event that will benefit the entire student body?
   d. Should it be allowed because no student is forced to buy a candy bar? If the price is too high, students can choose not to buy, which will lead the SGO to lower its prices or stop selling this item.
2. Alison visits thrift stores and purchases inexpensive jewelry. She cleans the pieces and takes them apart. She then reassembles them to form new pieces of jewelry.
   a. Is Alison behaving ethically only if she charges a small percentage more than the components cost her?
   b. Is Alison behaving ethically if she charges whatever she believes the market will bear?
3. Monique lost her hair when she underwent chemotherapy. After she recovered, based on her experiences, she opened a business selling wigs, hats, and scarves, targeting cancer patients as her market.
   a. If Monique sets her business up as a nonprofit and solicits donations and supporters so that she can supply her wares for free or at cost value, is she behaving more nobly than if she runs her business for profit?

b. Should Monique feel guilty if her for-profit store becomes successful, and she makes more than a minimal living from it?

c. Should Monique be shamed by her customers and the community for capitalizing on someone else's misfortune?

Write down any thoughts you have in the following box.

Activity 30.3 Guided Reflection and Action Plan

1. Review your thoughts after completing Exercise 30.2. Share both Secret #30 and this exercise with a peer. Discuss your reactions.
2. Consider the concept of money as a representation of service. Think about the times when you earned money in exchange for providing a service or product to others. Did naming the price for your service make you uncomfortable?
3. Consider the story of Grandpa Lapin and the process of creating wealth through economic transactions. How does this story resonate with your own experiences? Are there ways you can apply this understanding to your personal financial decisions?

Action Plan

1. Seek opportunities to think through why the cost of something you are purchasing is more than the cost of its components or what you might pay for it if you tracked it to its source.
2. Express gratitude to merchants for making it so easy for you to buy what you wish in pleasant surroundings.
3. Recognize the effort you put into your business activities and realize that others are putting in great effort to theirs as well, which is reflected in the prices they charge.
4. Stop yourself from buying something if you are going to be resentful because you think you are being overcharged. Either don't buy the item or think through the transaction and see if the price is actually a fair one.

Remember!

A proper transaction leaves both sides, the seller and the buyer, feeling that they are better off. Acquiring an object, preparing it for sale, marketing it, and selling it are actions that earn certificates of performance—otherwise known as money.

Summary and Encouragement

This chapter emphasizes the importance of understanding money and its role in our lives. Money is literally brought into existence when individuals serve one another, resulting in a cycle of prosperity within the economy. By understanding money's role in facilitating transactions, you become better equipped to attract and accumulate wealth.

Aligning your actions with an understanding of how money is created will open the doors to financial prosperity. Trust in the process of economic interactions and your ability to create wealth through service. Move forward with confidence and purpose, knowing that you have the tools to attract that which you best understand—money and the bountiful blessings it can bring into your life.

Secret #31

You Must Know Your Money, Which You Must Be Able to Measure and Count

In this essential chapter on your journey to financial empowerment, we lay out the importance of being financially literate. Just as losing weight requires a scale to measure your progress, building wealth necessitates a system for tracking and counting your financial growth.

The Hebrew language itself contains the idea that numbers and counting are important. It is no coincidence that each of five Biblical Hebrew words for counting also signify a person of substance.

You might think you're not a "numbers person," but you have the power to choose who you become. Just as you tackle challenges in other areas of your life, you can become financially literate and confident in handling financial statements.

Financial empowerment is within your reach. With dedication, knowledge, and the right tools, you'll confidently navigate the realm of finance and build a prosperous future.

Exercise 31.1

Your mission is to navigate through the maze, following the sequence of letters that make up the title, from the letter Y to the letter T, to find your way out.

1. Begin at the letter "Y" indicated as the maze's starting point.
2. Trace the path through the maze by following the sequence of letters in the title "You Must Know Your Money, Which You Must Be Able to Measure and Count."
3. Move through each letter in the exact order they appear in the title.
4. Continue tracing the path until you reach the letter "T" at the end of the title.

Solution:

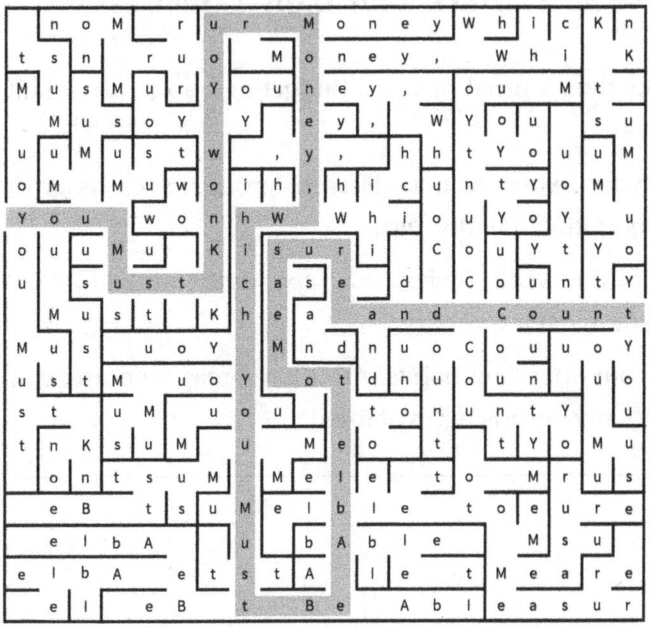

Exercise 31.2 Track Your Daily Expenses

1. Create a spending journal or use a budgeting app to record all your expenses for one week.
2. Categorize your expenses into different groups, such as groceries, entertainment, transportation, charity, etc.
3. At the end of the week, review your spending journal and calculate the total amount spent in each category.
4. Reflect on your spending habits. Are there areas where you should cut back? Did you find any surprising expenses?

Exercise 31.3 Share Your Financial Journey

1. Find someone who is savvier than you when it comes to money.
2. Discuss your financial goals, challenges, and successes with them.
3. Seek advice or feedback from this person and consider their perspective.
4. Write down what you learned from this meeting.

Activity 31.4 Guided Reflection and Action Plan

1. Think about your current approach to money management. Are you actively tracking your expenses and savings, or do you find it challenging to keep a record?
2. Consider the importance of counting and measuring your money. How does having a clear understanding of your financial situation empower you to make better decisions?
3. What are your financial goals? Are they specific and achievable, or do they need to be refined and better defined?
4. Consider your willingness to learn and improve your financial literacy. Are you open to gaining new knowledge and skills in managing your money?

Action Plan

1. Start Tracking Your Expenses:
    - Commit to keeping a spending journal or using a budgeting app to record all your expenses for the next month.
    - Categorize your expenses to gain insights into your spending patterns.
    - Review your spending journal regularly to identify areas where you should make improvements.
2. Create a Personal Balance Sheet:
    - List all your assets and liabilities to understand your net worth.
    - Update your balance sheet periodically to track your financial progress.
    - Analyze your balance sheet to identify opportunities for financial growth and debt reduction.

3. Set Specific Financial Goals:
   - Define clear and measurable financial objectives for the short, medium, and long term.
   - Break down each goal into actionable steps with deadlines.
   - Create a timeline for achieving your goals and regularly monitor your progress.
4. Improve Your Financial Literacy:
   - Take the initiative to learn about reading and interpreting financial statements.
   - Use online resources, books, or seek guidance from financial advisors to understand complex financial concepts.
   - Practice reading financial statements regularly to enhance your financial literacy.
5. Implement and Stick to a Budget:
   - Assess your income and expenses to create a realistic monthly budget.
   - Set spending limits for each category and aim to stay within those limits.
   - Review and adjust your budget as needed to maintain financial discipline.
6. Explore Investment Opportunities:
   - Research different investment options and understand their potential risks and returns.
   - Consider your financial goals and risk tolerance when selecting investments.
   - Develop an investment plan based on your analysis and consult with a financial advisor if required.

Remember!

With consistent effort and a proactive approach, you will gain better control over your finances.

Summary and Encouragement

This chapter emphasizes the importance of understanding, measuring, and counting our money. Monitoring our finances is crucial to achieving financial success. Counting and measuring our money provides tangible evidence of our financial progress, which motivates us to continue making wise financial decisions.

The chapter also emphasizes the significance of financial literacy and the need to be actively involved in managing our money. Learning to read and interpret financial statements is essential to making informed decisions about investments, savings, and expenses. We should not shy away from financial matters just because we may not consider ourselves "numbers people." With commitment and effort, anyone can master basic financial concepts and take control of their financial affairs.

Take pride in your commitment to financial literacy and make a conscious effort to understand your financial situation better. As you actively manage your money, you will gain confidence in your abilities and make better informed decisions that align with your goals.

Take charge of your finances, learn from the past, and plan for a prosperous future. Count your blessings, count your savings, and count on yourself to create a brighter financial future. With dedication and determination, you can achieve financial freedom and fulfill your dreams.

Secret #32

Money Is Spiritual

Throughout this book, we have introduced the idea that money symbolizes participation in the economy and serves as a token of our service to others. As we've learned, money is both a reward for serving God's children and a motivator to continue doing so.

Now it's time to take our understanding to a deeper level and discover what's at stake when we recognize money as spiritual. By weaving together the biblical business secrets you've already learned, we create a unified theory of money that reflects its spiritual essence.

Unlike a physical object that can only be in one place at a time, the value represented by money flows through the economy, impacting multiple lives simultaneously. The spiritual aspect of money is infinite and has the potential to create exponential wealth.

This perspective challenges the false notion that money is finite and can only be obtained by taking it away from others. In contrast, we see how making ourselves richer can benefit everyone and foster growth in the economy. As we explore the distinction between money as a physical object and money as a spiritual construct, we uncover the truth behind economic theories and the importance of a thriving market economy.

Furthermore, we address the importance of understanding money's critical role in our lives. Money is not merely a means of exchange; it represents the entire aggregate of our time, effort, and dedication. This perspective empowers us to make wiser financial decisions and attract more wealth through our service to others.

Exercise 32.1

Fill in the crossword puzzle with the key concepts we have covered. Each key concept corresponds to a unique definition.

Crossword Puzzle

Across

3. The increase in the general price level of goods and services in an economy over time, resulting in a decrease in the purchasing power of money.

6. Having limits or boundaries, measurable and constrained.

8. The decrease in the general price level of goods and services in an economy, causing an increase in the purchasing power of money.

9. Relating to the nonphysical or metaphysical aspects of life, encompassing values, beliefs, and principles.

10. An economic system in which the price of goods and services is determined by supply and demand without significant government intervention.

Down

1. Officially recognized currency or coins that can be used to settle debts and obligations.
2. Limitless or boundless, without an endpoint or restriction.
4. A socioeconomic system where the means of production, distribution, and exchange are owned or regulated by the government.
5. Pertaining to the tangible, material world and objects that can be perceived through the senses.
7. The representation of wealth in the form of currency, coins, or digital transactions, serving as a medium of exchange in economic transactions.

Solution:

Exercise 32.2 Growth Moments

1. As you hear or read about business or government financial policies, etc., ask yourself if the people involved see money as purely materialistic or do they see that there is a spiritual component.
2. Research the idea of Universal Basic Income. Does reading this chapter cause you to view it from a different perspective?
3. Write a letter to the editor of a newspaper that has published an article with a throw-away line describing business owners as motivated by greed.

Exercise 32.3 Infinite Wealth Creation

1. Think of a product or service that you use or consume regularly. It could be a smartphone, a streaming service, a food delivery app, food, transport, etc.
2. In writing, describe the ways in which this product or service has created value for you and how it has contributed to wealth creation within the economy.
3. Consider the ripple effects of this product or service on other businesses, job opportunities, and overall economic growth.

Exercise 32.4 Money as Life Force Visualization

1. Make a 20-minute appointment with yourself and put it on your calendar. Keep it.
2. Think of an object of some value that you have recently purchased. Carefully assess how much time it took you to be able to afford that object.
3. Imagine sitting in a waiting room for that amount of time and having the office close for the day before you are ever seen.
4. What would you feel as you left the office, having wasted so much of your time?
5. Does this help you value the time that you put into acquiring the previously mentioned object?

Activity 32.5 Guided Reflection and Action Plan

Step 1: Personal Beliefs

Do you instinctively view money as finite or infinite? Do you approach money from a scarcity mindset, being fearful of poverty if you spend it or give it away?

Step 2: Relationship with Money

Explore your personal relationship with money. Do you see it merely as a physical object, or can you recognize its spiritual nature as a representation of your time, effort, and contributions to society? How might acknowledging money's spiritual aspect influence your financial decisions?

Action Plan

Step 1: Setting Intentions

Based on your reflections, set clear intentions about how you want to approach money and wealth creation in the future.

Step 2: Aligning Actions

Identify specific actions you can take to align your financial decisions with your newfound understanding of money's spirituality.

Step 3: Reflecting on Progress

Regularly review your progress in implementing your action plan. Assess how your beliefs and actions around money have evolved and what positive changes you have experienced. Make any necessary adjustments to your approach.

Step 4: Sharing Insights

Engage in discussions with friends, family, or colleagues about the concepts explored in this chapter. Share your insights, learn from others' perspectives, and encourage open dialogue about the spiritual nature of money.

Remember!

Align your beliefs and actions with principles delineated in this chapter and create a more purposeful and fulfilling relationship with money.

Summary and Encouragement

The chapter emphasizes the spiritual nature of money. The distinction between physical legal tender and money as a spiritual construct is crucial to understanding its infinite and transformative potential.

We challenge the belief that money is finite and, instead, encourage seeing money as an infinite resource capable of coming into being through the magic of economic interaction. The concept of money as spiritual is further reinforced by the fact that no machine can measure value. That is something that requires two human beings. In times of financial challenges or uncertainty, holding onto the belief that money is not finite makes it easier to find new ways to create wealth.

Secret #33

How You Feel About Yourself Is How Others Will See You

Just as you can intuit the emotions and feelings of others, people can also pick up on your self-perception and emotions, which ultimately shapes their opinion of you. Secret #33 discusses the power of positive self-perception and its impact on our personal and professional lives. If you feel tarnished by earning money, your views will hinder your success and create barriers in your relationships with customers, colleagues, and business partners.

By cultivating a positive and self-assured mindset, you set yourself on a path to professional growth and fulfillment.

Exercise 33.1

Carefully scan the grid horizontally, vertically, and diagonally. Look for the words listed in the following key terms section. When you find a word, circle or mark it to highlight its location. Letters may be used in more than one word and may read in all directions. Take your time and enjoy the challenge! Find all nine words.

T	R	U	S	T	W	O	R	T	H	Y	P	M	E
Y	E	A	F	U	L	F	I	L	L	M	E	N	T
H	S	R	D	E	S	E	R	V	I	N	G	A	R
T	P	E	P	I	F	U	L	F	I	L	L	M	U
A	E	S	O	F	A	U	T	H	E	N	T	I	C
P	C	P	O	S	I	T	I	V	E	A	U	T	O
M	T	I	V	E	S	R	E	S	P	O	N	D	N
E	R	A	D	I	T	N	E	D	I	F	N	O	C
S	E	L	F	A	S	S	U	R	E	D	E	S	E

Words to Find

- *Trustworthy*
- *Confident*
- *Self-assured*
- *Deserving*
- *Authentic*
- *Respect*
- *Positive*
- *Fulfillment*
- *Radiate*

Exercise 33.2 Reflect on Your Self-perception

1. How do you feel about yourself in various aspects of your life, including personal, professional, and financial?
2. Write down your honest thoughts and emotions about your self-worth, confidence, and moral standing.
3. Consider how these feelings may affect your interactions with others, such as customers, business partners, colleagues, and friends.
4. Note any negative or self-limiting beliefs that might be influencing your behavior and communication with others.

Exercise 33.3

1. Think of a time when you were impressed with another person's work. Perhaps you had an outstanding meal in a restaurant, a gardener beautified an area, or a lawyer negotiated a difficult settlement.
2. Recognize what that person's talents and efforts added to your life.
3. Articulate those thoughts in complete sentences.
4. Now picture someone else thanking you for what you do.
5. Articulate those thoughts in complete sentences.

Exercise 33.4

Practice asking for a raise or bonus. Even if you are in business for yourself, get into a conversation with yourself.

1. Make a list of how your work has benefited the business.
2. What strengths and characteristics do you bring to the company?
3. Why does it make sense for your boss to raise your salary?
4. Practice enumerating your achievements without sounding boastful.
5. Can you commit to adding a skill set in order to make yourself more valuable?

Activity 33.5 Guided Reflection and Action Plan

1. How do your beliefs impact your self-perception and behavior in social and business settings?
2. Have there been instances where you knew that your self-perception was influencing how others perceived you? How did your feelings about yourself affect the outcomes of these interactions?
3. Consider moments when you projected confidence and authenticity. How did you feel about yourself during those times, and how did others respond to your positive self-image?

Action Plan

1. Set Positive Intentions: Before important interactions, articulate the validity of your vision. Visualize successful and harmonious interactions where you leave a positive impression on others.
2. Address Self-Limiting Beliefs: Recognize and challenge self-limiting beliefs that hinder your ability to project a positive self-image. Question the validity of these beliefs and provide evidence of your achievements and strengths.
3. Monitor Your Progress: Maintain a record in your journal tracking your progress in projecting a positive self-perception. Do you see positive changes in how others respond to you and how you feel during these interactions?

Remember!

Others will largely see you as you see yourself. Understand the genuine value in what you do and how you are making life better for many other people with your work.

Summary and Encouragement

Secret #33 explores the profound connection between how we feel about ourselves and how others perceive us. It emphasizes that our self-perception has a significant impact on our interactions with others, especially in business settings. When we radiate positivity, confidence, and authenticity, and know that we are adding value to people's lives, others are naturally drawn to us and more willing to engage in meaningful relationships. Conversely, negative self-perception can hinder our success and create barriers in our professional and personal life.

Secret #34

The Surprising Benefits of Charity

At first glance, it may seem counterintuitive that giving money away is an important step in being open to making more money, but as we explore the ancient Jewish wisdom and principles presented in this chapter, we discover the truth behind this idea.

Generously and wisely giving away our money is not just a religious act. It also has the power to transform our perception of ourselves. Stretching our "giving muscles" makes us more capable of investing our time, energy, and money in building a business.

As you progress through the workbook activities and guided reflections in this chapter, recognize that the act of giving not only enriches the lives of others but also brings immeasurable richness to your own life.

Exercise 34.1

Test your understanding of the key concepts from the chapter. For each pair of sentences, mark the correct one and cross out the incorrect one.

1a. Giving back to society is an important activity for those in business.

1b. Giving is an important activity for those in business.

2a. Giving money away to help people in need has been shown to assist both psychological and physical health.

2b. Giving money away to help people in need adds stress to our lives.

3a. We often need to be comfortable in giving mode before we open to being comfortable in a receiving mode.

3b. It is foolish to expend money or effort without a guaranteed return.

4a. Keeping a tight hold on your money is the best way to ensure that your bank account grows.

4b. Counterintuitively, we should be comfortable giving charity even when our own bank account is smaller than we would like.

5a. Companies benefit when they offer something for free to potential customers.

5b. Companies should expect customers to put money on the table before serving them.

6a. Pipes and tubes are bidirectional.

6b. When you open a channel, it only allows things to flow in one direction.

Answer Key

These are the correct statements:

1b; 2a; 3a; 4b; 5a; 6a

Exercise 34.2 Discovering Your Giving Beliefs

Our attitudes toward money and giving to charity are shaped by our families, our cultures, and our histories. What is your starting point? Use the following box to jot down any thoughts that may arise.

- Was giving to charity a staple of your childhood home?
- When you received money as a gift or an allowance, were you trained to give some of it away to charity?
- Were you aware of your parents regularly donating to organizations they supported?
- Was your home open to those in need? For example, were guests such as widows or widowers, or those alone for any reason, invited to join your holiday celebrations?
- Did you frequently hear statements betraying jealousy and resentment of those who had more than you?

Exercise 34.3 Guided Reflection and Action Plan

Use the following questions to guide your reflection.

1. Has this chapter challenged or changed your perspective on giving and wealth?
2. What role does generosity play in your life currently and how does it make you feel?
3. Consider the impact of your charitable actions on others and how it affects their perception of you. How does this align with your desired personal and professional image?
4. Reflect on any experiences where you felt a strong connection with a cause or organization you supported. How did that sense of purpose and alignment affect your giving experience?
5. Do you tend to give thoughtfully, vetting where or to whom you are giving, or do you give impulsively when your heartstrings are tugged?
6. Which style of giving do you want to follow?

Action Plan

Now that you have reflected on the chapter's key concepts, create an action plan to cultivate generosity and experience the feeling of wealth through giving.

1. Define Your Philanthropic Vision:
   - Write down your philanthropic goals and the causes you feel passionate about supporting.
   - Identify specific organizations or initiatives that align with your values and resonate with you.

- Conduct thorough research on the organizations you wish to support.
- By paying attention to transparency and accountability in the operation of charities, ensure that your contribution is making a meaningful difference.

2. Set Giving Goals:

- Determine a percentage of your income or resources that you will allocate to charitable giving.
- Set monthly giving targets to measure your progress and impact.

3. Practice Giving:

- If you are not accustomed to giving, allocate a container that is dedicated to a specific cause. Place a dollar a day in the container and donate it at the end of the month. The repeated action of placing money in the container will be more valuable than taking $30 out of your pocket at one time.
- At the end of the month, ask yourself if your daily giving has had an emotional impact on you.

4. Become Aware of Anti-wealth Sentiments:

- If you are engaged in honest and ethical work, do not give to charity out of guilt.
- If you are approached to "give back to society," correct that statement, preferably to the person making it but at a minimum out loud to yourself.

5. Monitor and Adjust:

- Review your giving goals semi-annually.
- Adjust your action plan as needed to accommodate changes.

6. Integrate Giving into Your Daily Life:

- Practice giving not only financially but also through acts of service, kindness, and compassion.

Remember!

The act of giving to charity is valuable in and of itself. As a bonus, being a giving person and thinking of yourself as such sets you up for success in business.

Summary and Encouragement

- This chapter explores the powerful connection between generosity and feeling wealthy. The concept may seem paradoxical at first, but giving money away does indeed make us feel abundant and prosperous. Giving is not just a selfless act; it is also a path to personal growth and a positive self-perception.
- Strengthening our giving muscles allows us to be more assertive in business. When we are comfortable with giving, we are able to invest in ourselves and our businesses, confident that we will be on the receiving end down the road.
- Generosity and philanthropy play a significant role in how others perceive us and how we perceive ourselves. When we give selflessly, we project an image of success and abundance. People are naturally drawn to those who are charitable and compassionate, creating valuable connections in both personal and professional settings.

Secret #35

Giving Money Away Automatically Connects Us with Other People

Participating in acts of charity assists us in building meaningful connections. Being part of a congregation or a charitable organization strengthens our sense of accountability and shared purpose, making us less likely to engage in negative behaviors. It also provides networking opportunities that can profoundly impact our personal and professional lives.

By actively engaging in charity, we connect with like-minded, virtuous individuals who share our values and goals. These connections are not superficial but often lead to genuine friendships and collaborations.

The concept of giving and taking is deeply rooted in human interactions and is exemplified through one of the Hebrew words for friendship that holds within it a universal symbol of friendship—the handshake. Friendship involves both giving and taking. The story told in the chapter of competitors rallying around to support each other when one of them hits a rough patch is neither unusual nor unique.

Be part of a community, share your blessings, and experience the profound connections that arise when you relate to others with an open heart.

Exercise 35.1

Decide if the following statements are true or false.

1. People should keep their business and social lives separate from each other.
2. It is wrong to do business with those one meets in religious or charitable situations.
3. Business competitors should seek to destroy each other.
4. When you present an image of yourself as an honorable and successful entrepreneur, others tend to feel positive about you.
5. Retail therapy gives short-lived pleasure.

Answers:

1. False; 2. False; 3. False; 4. True; 5. True

Exercise 35.2 Reflections—Importance of Connections and Charity

Write freely in the space provided, responding to the following prompts.

1. How have most of your friendships been formed? Are they old school and childhood chums or have you made friends as an adult through religious and charitable associations?
2. Do you decide what organization you wish to belong to based more, less, or equally on who else belongs, on the purpose and essence of the group, or for pragmatic reasons?
3. Think about the charitable organizations you are familiar with. How do they contribute to the well-being of the community, and what role do connections play in their success?
4. Do you think of charity as something you will do once you have made your fortune?

Exercise 35.3 Guided Reflection and Action Plan

Reflection Questions

1. How do you currently prioritize building connections with others in your life? Are there specific areas, such as personal, professional, or community relationships, where you feel the need to improve?
2. Have you experienced the joy and fulfillment that comes from giving to charity or helping others in need?
3. Have you ever had the opportunity to behave benevolently to a competitor or coworker? How did this affect your relationship and your professional life?

Action Plan

1. Be a Giver: Identify charitable organizations or causes that resonate with you and volunteer your time or resources to support them. Whether it's donating to a local charity, participating in community service projects, or organizing fundraising events, giving enriches both your life and the lives of others.
2. Practice Empathy: Develop your ability to empathize with others by actively listening to their stories and perspectives. Put yourself in their shoes to better understand their challenges and needs. Empathy strengthens connections and fosters compassion.
3. Join Supportive Groups: Seek out groups or communities that align with your values and interests. Being part of a supportive group can provide a sense of belonging and offer opportunities for personal growth.

Remember!

Giving to charity is both admirable and desirable on many levels. Don't discount the benefit that the giver gets from associating with others who share his or her values.

Summary and Encouragement

This chapter emphasizes that forming meaningful relationships that are vital for the well-being of the community and essential for personal growth, professional success, and overall fulfillment can be accessed through involvement with appropriate charities.

Recognize the potential of building connections through charitable activities. Take the time to nurture and deepen your relationships with others, as they will form a crucial support network during life's challenges and celebrations.

Remember that charity is not limited to financial contributions; it involves sharing your time, skills, and compassion with others. Give freely and generously and witness the incredible impact you can have on the lives of others and your own.

Secret #36

Ideas Hit Reality

Just as there are fads in clothing, in vacation spots, and in foods, fads pop up in the business world. Sometimes, these new ideas become entrenched as they prove their value. Unfortunately, sometimes the ideas are terrible and hobble the aspiring entrepreneur and prevent business professionals from being successful.

Secret #36 shows that just as a drop of poison can ruin a huge batch of soup, one terrible idea can destroy an entire enterprise. The chapter encourages awareness so that you won't be felled by a fad. While it is impossible to mention every bad idea that is currently out there or to predict what might be coming down the road, these workbook exercises are designed to stimulate your skepticism muscle and motivate you not to be one of the crowd when the crowd resembles nothing so much as a bunch of lemmings heading toward the edge of a cliff.

Exercise 36.1 Pro or Con?

Read the following ideas, some of which are based on actual fads and some of which are imaginary. For each example, write three questions that you would ask if you were the business professional in charge of deciding whether to implement or not to implement these ideas.

1. Convert the current office space, which consists of individual offices, into an open plan office where everyone works in a large, shared space.

1.
2.
3.

2. Introduce 45 minutes of physical exercise at the start of every workday, based on the idea that the healthier workers are, the more productive they will be.

1.
2.
3.

3. Provide a bonus to any employee who does not miss any days of work over a three-month period.

1.
2.
3.

Exercise 36.2 Draw the Circle

Make a list of the qualities you would want to find in a spouse, friend, coworker, or employee. Put down between six and ten points. In the second column write one quality that would make the first list entirely irrelevant. Bonus: Write down a number of other qualities that would negate the first list.

1. 2. 3. 4. 5. 6. 7. 8. 9. 10.	1.

Exercise 36.3 Guided Reflection and Action Plan

- Think about your personal lifestyle when it comes to clothing, popular music, social media usage, etc. How quick are you to adopt new trends? Do you tend to jump in and evaluate later, or do you hold back and see how things play out?
- Have you ever made a major life decision based on the latest psychological findings? How did that play out for you?
- Review your sources of acquiring news. Do you read articles across the business and political spectrum, or do you limit your information gathering only to those podcasts, newspapers, and magazines that agree with your views?
- How comfortable are you with going against the crowd? Are you able to maintain your own standards while still retaining cordial relationships with others who think differently from you?

Action Plan

1. Expand Your Thinking: Practice making pro and con lists when facing decisions.
2. Engage in Debate: Pick a lighthearted, noncontroversial, even whimsical topic (for example: We should recommend a local ordinance stating that all stores on Main Street should have flower boxes outside their storefronts). Find a friend or family member to debate the topic. Then reverse sides and argue for the opposite point.
3. Strengthen Your Spine:. No one appreciates someone who is unnecessarily pugilistic, stubborn, and nonconforming. Yet, each of us needs to have the ability to draw a line in the sand when we uphold a position no matter who disagrees with us. Put down in writing what your lines in the sand are.

Remember!

Ideas can spread as easily as germs can. The wrong idea at the wrong time can negate all the hard work you put into developing your business or professional self. Be aware of this danger.

Summary and Encouragement

While much of this book focuses on establishing relationships with others, being a part of a group, and the benefits that accrue from being part of a team, Secret #36, "Ideas Hit Reality," cautions against mindlessly going along with groupthink. Especially because of the speed and reach that social media provides, ideas can spread rapidly and intensely.

New ideas can be beneficial, but they also can be foolish. We all need to develop the tools that allow us to evaluate ideas, regardless of how strongly they are being presented. Being a person of strong character and discernment is an aid in making money and acquiring wealth. Take the necessary steps to be such an individual!

Secret #37

If There Is No Hebrew Word for Something, Then That Thing Does Not Exist

In this chapter, we explore an intriguing concept that challenges our understanding of certain words and ideas in the English language. We begin with a tale of adventure on the high seas that leads us to a profound realization about the significance of certain words and their implications in our lives. Secret #37 takes us on a thought-provoking journey into the world of words and their meanings, specifically exploring the absence of certain words in ancient Hebrew.

This chapter may challenge your assumptions and provide a new perspective that could lead you to question some previously unquestioned ideas.

Exercise 37.1

For each of the following statements, indicate whether it is true or false.

____________________ 1. The sailing journey took place in the Atlantic Ocean.

____________________ 2. The English word "right" is meaningless.

____________________ 3. If a word does not exist in biblical Hebrew, we should question whether the concept it represents exists.

____________________ 4. Modern Hebrew has no words for technological inventions such as "telephone" or "helicopter."

____________________ 5. "Fairness" is an ancient and important idea.

____________________ 6. Retirement has been present in societies for centuries.

____________________ 7. The notion of entitlement is supported in the Bible.

____________________ 8. Coincidences are God's way of camouflaging His involvement in the world.

____________________ 9. There are no implications from the British use of the word *holiday* versus the American use of the word *vacation*.

Answers:

1. False; 2. True; 3. True; 4. False; 5. False; 6. False; 7. False; 8. True; 9. False

Exercise 37.2 Personal Obligations

1. List three personal obligations you take upon yourself.
2. Write a few words detailing each obligation.
3. List three personal obligations that someone else in your life takes upon themselves regarding you.
4. How is your behavior affected by not thinking either you or anyone else has a right to these actions?
   a. Reflect on the impact of these obligations.

Exercise 37.3 Coincidence Versus Purpose

1. Recall personal experiences you might have labeled as "coincidences" in the past.
2. How might you view these coincidences as moments of purpose?
3. How might viewing coincidences in this way affect your life?

Exercise 37.4 Imagining Life Without Retirement

1. Envision a world where retirement doesn't exist.
2. Explore the societal structure, career paths, and life stages.
3. What are the implications of a life that doesn't have retirement as a goal?
4. If society eliminated retirement, would one consequence be a shortage of jobs?

Exercise 37.5 Guided Reflection and Action Plan

1. Consider the concept of "rights" as discussed in the chapter. Think about a situation where you have felt that you had a right to something. Reflect on whether that right was truly guaranteed and who had the obligation to provide you with that right.

2. Explore your perspective on retirement. Do you believe in the traditional concept of retirement? Consider how work, service, and contribution play a role in your life, both now and in the future.

Action Plan

1. Evaluate Your Rights and Obligations: Identify areas in your life where you feel entitled to certain things or rights. Take a moment to reevaluate these beliefs and consider whether there are corresponding obligations that come with those rights. Take proactive steps to fulfill your obligations and avoid expecting entitlements.

2. Seek Purpose in Everyday Events: Going forward, look for purpose in events that might seem coincidental at first glance. Keep a journal to record these moments and reflect on any potential messages or lessons you can draw from them.

3. Redefine Retirement: Explore ways to stay engaged and productive throughout your life, even if it means transitioning to different roles or activities. Focus on finding fulfillment in serving others and contributing to society rather than seeking a "time for me" retirement.
4. Explore the Impact of Language: Take the time to explore other languages and cultures, paying attention to words and concepts that might not have direct translations in your native language. How does this impact the way people from different cultures perceive and interact with the world?

Remember!

Language matters! The words we use affect our thoughts and beliefs.

Summary and Encouragement

Secret #37, "If There Is No Hebrew Word for Something, Then That Thing Does Not Exist," takes us on a thought-provoking journey into the world of language and concepts. Drawing from personal experiences, biblical insights, and linguistic nuances, the chapter challenges us to reevaluate our understanding of certain English words like "rights," "retirement," and "fairness." The central idea is that the absence of direct biblical Hebrew equivalents for these words suggests they may not be accurate ideas. The chapter encourages us to shift our focus from "rights" to "obligations" and underscores the importance of continuous service and contribution throughout our lives.

As you engage with the activities in this workbook chapter and reflect on your personal obligations, where thoughts of entitlement may have crept into your psyche, your ideas about retirement, and even the concept of fairness, we hope that you are inspired to reshape your points of view to ones that lead you to feel grateful and expansive rather than entitled and limited.

Secret #38

Retirement Is Unhealthy

The notion that retirement may not be as beneficial as commonly believed is the crux of this chapter. It challenges the societal views that often glorify the idea of retiring at a certain age to enjoy leisure and relaxation and explores the potential negative impacts of retirement on our physical, emotional, and spiritual well-being.

Many of us look forward to the day when we can retire and bid farewell to the daily grind. We envision a time of freedom and relaxation, where we can pursue our interests and hobbies without the demands of a job. However, Secret #38 presents a different perspective—one that urges us to reconsider the idea of retirement and its potential consequences.

Exercise 38.1

Match the key terms and concepts from the chapter with their corresponding descriptions.

1. The act of ceasing work and enjoying leisure after reaching a certain age

2. Being answerable for one's actions and responsibilities

3. Engaging in unpaid work to support a cause or organization

4. A sense of meaning and direction in life

5. The practice of adhering to rules and order to achieve goals

6. Company policies that do not allow workers to continue past a certain age

A. Discipline

B. Forced retirement

C. Volunteering

D. Accountability

E. Purpose

F. Retirement

Answers:

1. F; 2. D; 3. C; 4. E; 5. A; 6. B

Exercise 38.2 Retirement Letter to Your Future Self

Write a heartfelt letter to your future self, focusing on your later years. Follow these steps.

1. Take a few moments to clear your mind and focus on the concept of retirement. Ask yourself the following questions:
   - What are your main aspirations as you get older?
   - How do you envision maintaining physical, emotional, and spiritual well-being?
   - What family, service, or community involvement goals do you have?
   - Are there specific activities or projects you want to engage in if you do have more free time?
   - Consider your unique dreams, desires, and intentions for this stage of life.
2. Begin writing your letter to your future self.
   - Address the letter to yourself as if you are writing to a dear friend. Be sincere and open in your writing.
   - Share your thoughts and feelings about growing older, the experiences you hope to have, and the contributions you still wish to make.
   - Emphasize the importance of continuing to serve others.
3. Take a moment to reread what you've written. Reflect on the significance of your goals and intentions.
   - Store your letter in a safe place. Write down where you put it. No matter how obvious the location is to you now, you may not remember it in the future.
4. Choose a date down the road when you wish to revisit your letter. This might be one year from now, at which point you may wish to update the letter. Alternatively, it might be 30 years down the road when the contents will be more applicable. Put a tickler in your calendar for when you wish to read it.

5. On the chosen date, open the letter and reflect on how your journey aligns with your initial aspirations and goals. Use this moment to rekindle your motivation and make any adjustments needed.

Exercise 38.3 Interview with a Retiree

Interview a few retired individuals about their experiences after retirement. Gently ask about their physical and mental health, if they stayed engaged in their career field, and how they spend their time.

Exercise 38.4 Inspirational Role Models

Identify inspirational role models who have continued to serve others and make a difference well into their older years. Write down your thoughts about their experiences. You may also create presentations or posters to showcase these individuals and their contributions to society.

Exercise 38.5 Guided Reflection and Action Plan

1. How do you currently view retirement? Do you see it as a time of rest and relaxation? Do you worry about its potential effects on your well-being?
2. Have you witnessed any examples of retirees experiencing decline in health or a sense of worthlessness after retiring? Do these experiences affect your perspective on retirement?
3. Do you find it difficult to imagine stopping work?
4. Consider the connection between purpose and health. How might maintaining a sense of purpose and service impact your overall well-being?

Action Plan

Use the following steps to guide your planning.

Step 1: Define Your Purpose

- Write down your passions, skills, and interests. Consider how you can leverage these qualities even after retiring from a traditional career.

Step 2: Explore Opportunities

- Research various opportunities for part-time jobs or teaching and mentoring opportunities that align with your interests and skills. Look for ways to participate in causes or organizations you are passionate about.

Step 3: Set Goals

- Establish specific and measurable goals for your life as you age. These goals should include both personal growth objectives and ways to serve others.

Step 4: Develop a Schedule

- If you are no longer working full time, create a weekly or monthly schedule that includes activities related to your goals.

Remember!

Getting older does not mean the end of serving others. Plan on staying active, both physically and mentally by continuing to work, even if the type of work you do changes.

Summary and Encouragement

Secret #38, "Retirement Is Unhealthy," challenges the conventional notion of retirement and explores its potential negative impact on physical, emotional, and spiritual well-being. The chapter shares anecdotes of retirees experiencing declines in health and a sense of worthlessness after leaving the workforce. Retirement can lead to a lack of purpose and accountability, resulting in a loss of drive and fulfillment. The chapter emphasizes the importance of serving others and maintaining a sense of purpose throughout life.

Secret #39

How You Think About Tomorrow Affects How You Behave Today

Too often, we let nagging thoughts about tomorrow overshadow our present, affecting our emotional and spiritual well-being. This chapter challenges us to reconsider the significance of our actions and decisions in shaping our lives and destinies.

In this chapter, we discuss how misplaced planning for the future can corrupt our present, impacting our relationships, career choices, and overall sense of purpose. This includes wrong ideas about retirement, raising questions about the common practice of planning to withdraw from active service once we've earned enough money.

Using insightful examples, "How You Think about Tomorrow Affects How You Behave Today" encourages us to shift our perspective on planning for the future and reevaluate the true essence of work.

Exercise 39.1 Looking Down the Road

1. List three areas where having a picture that encompasses past, present, and future changes how you act. For example: When parents have a clear picture of the adults that they hope their children will become, they raise those children differently than if their major concern is the child's happiness only in the here and now. Another example: If you are aware of deficits in your knowledge bank that deter you from applying for a position you desire, you can choose to fill in that gap and move forward.

1.
2.
3.

Exercise 39.2 Pointless Worrying About the Future

Take some time to reflect on your own experiences when worrying about the future has impacted your present. Use the following space to jot down your thoughts.

1. Recall a specific instance when worrying about the future affected your ability to fully enjoy and engage in the present.
2. Did the situation that worried you come to be? If so, were there other times that your worry turned out to be unfounded?
3. The heroic World War II resistance figure and devout Christian, Corrie ten Boom, said, "Worry does not empty tomorrow of its sorrow. It empties today of its strength." Do you agree?

Exercise 39.3 Reframing Your Actions

We all engage in repetitious or persnickety tasks, or ones that irritate us. Recognizing how they fit into a higher purpose can change our attitude. Find a higher purpose in each of the listed situations.

1. Tedious paperwork must be filled in each time a large sale is made.
2. You are sitting in traffic on the way to an in-person meeting that could have been a Zoom call.
3. A bakery apprentice being told to redo a cake because the color of the frosting was one shade too light.
4. A student received an F on a paper because his personal information was not filled in correctly.

Exercise 39.4 Guided Reflection and Action Plan

1. Reflect on Your Current Mindset: Take a moment to evaluate your current mindset regarding the future and how it affects your present. Are you often preoccupied with worries about what might happen tomorrow, next week, or in the distant future? Consider how this mindset impacts your emotional well-being and sense of fulfillment in your daily life.
2. Examine Your Career Goals: Think about your career goals and future plans. Does your current career path align with your higher purpose and values?
3. Set Present-Focused Goals: Identify specific goals that will help you shift your focus to the present. These goals could include practicing mindfulness techniques, being more attentive to the needs of others, and seeking opportunities to contribute positively to your workplace or community.
4. Define Your Higher Purpose: How would you describe your work in a way that motivates others to wish to join you?

Remember!

You gain a deeper understanding of the impact of the past and the future by regularly reflecting on and reviewing your current activities. Keep the bigger picture in mind and make sure that you are aware of the nobility of the work you do each day.

Summary and Encouragement

Secret #39, "How You Think About Tomorrow Affects How You Behave Today," emphasizes the detrimental effects of pointless worrying about the future and making negative plans. The chapter highlights that such thoughts can infect our present and hinder our ability to live fully in the moment. Drawing parallels from various aspects of life, the chapter argues that the future is interconnected with the present and the past. The discussion also delves into the significance of finding higher purpose in our actions and serving others rather than solely pursuing monetary gains.

You have the power to shape your future by keeping a bigger picture in mind that includes past, present, and future.

Secret #40

The Three Most Important Words: Relationships, Relationships, Relationships

As fewer individuals form families, participate in religious communities, and work side by side with others, many people are discovering that loneliness is a sad challenge. A thriving work-life is one of the ways in which we form meaningful relationships.

As individuals transition from their working lives to retirement, they may find themselves without the social networks that were once integral to their daily lives, such as coworkers, customers, and professional relationships. The absence of these connections can lead to a sense of isolation that impacts emotional well-being and overall life satisfaction.

In Secret #40, we look at the essence of friendship and affection, the power of mutual obligations, and the significance of forging deep and lasting connections with others. Both doing and receiving favors are ways to jumpstart relationships. The chapter also emphasizes the importance of being a valuable and indispensable member of one's professional community and how these strong bonds lead to a more fulfilled and purposeful life. Recognize that earning money is an important link in allowing people to allocate resources and live with one another in peace and friendship.

Exercise 40.1

Match the descriptions with key concepts that are related to this chapter.

1. Positive actions that people do for each other	a. *HaVeR*
2. What decent people feel a sense of when another person does something for them	b. Retention
3. A Hebrew word for friend, based on the root letters that mean obligation	c. Excellence
4. What everyone should strive to deliver as they work	d. Favors
5. The state of continually being by oneself	e. Isolation
6. When a business needs to hire new people because they have lost or let go of employees	f. Lottery
7. Businesses prefer this to hiring new employees	g. Money
8. A random way of apportioning money or goods	h. Friendship
9. A relationship based on voluntary mutual obligation	i. Obligation
10. One definition of this is as the aggregate of your time, skills, persistence, morality, and ability to build and maintain relationships	j. Turnover

Answers: *1. d; 2. i; 3. a; 4. c; 5. e; 6. j; 7. b; 8. f; 9. h; 10. g*

Exercise 40.2 Reflection Questions

a. Have you made meaningful connections through your workplace?

b. Can you recall any instances when doing a favor for someone or accepting a favor created stronger bonds between you and the other person? It might have been as simple as offering to pick up a coffee for a coworker or as profound as donating a kidney.

c. Are you more comfortable doing or receiving favors?

Exercise 40.3 Relationship Circle Analysis

Create a relationship circle to visualize the different groups of people you interact with regularly (e.g., coworkers, friends, family, community members). Assess the depth of your connections with each group and identify areas where you wish for more connection. Develop strategies to strengthen and expand your relationships within these circles.

Exercise 40.4

List the five ways mentioned in the chapter in which to allocate highly desirable resources such as rare waterfront property. Can you think of any other ways to do so? How many of these methods are used in various areas of your society ranging from government to the way your place of worship or social club operates?

Exercise 40.5 Guided Reflection and Action Plan

1. Relationships in the Working World:
   - Consider the relationships you have formed in your working life, whether with coworkers, clients, or business associates.
   - How do these connections differ from social interactions outside of work?
2. Value of Mutual Service:
   - Contemplate the concept of mutual favors and how it creates deeper bonds among individuals in professional settings.
3. Importance of Obligation in Friendship:
   - Review the source of the Hebrew word *H-V-R* and its meaning of friendship based on obligations.
   - Do you agree that obligations can intensify relationships and create a sense of connection and responsibility toward one another?
4. Your Role in Building Relationships:
   - Evaluate your role in building relationships with others, both in your professional and personal life.
   - Consider whether you actively seek opportunities to reach out to others and create bonds through mutual interactions.

Action Plan

1. Do Favors:
   - Commit to doing favors for others as a way to strengthen your relationship with them.
2. Journaling and Reflection:
   - Note in your journal when you attempt to initiate a relationship by doing or asking for a favor.
   - Observe whether your actions led to any changes.
3. Build Meaningful Connections:
   - Prioritize building meaningful connections with coworkers, clients, and other professional contacts.
   - Ensure that your work is excellent so that you are an important member of your work team.
4. Recognize the Value of Past Work Relationships:
   - Stay connected with former colleagues, mentors, and business associates, nurturing these connections.

Remember!

The bonds you create through serving others are the lifeblood of your relationships and the key to avoiding isolation in retirement or at any stage of life.

Summary and Encouragement

The chapter emphasizes the importance of doing favors for others and accepting favors in building and maintaining meaningful connections. This creates a bond of obligation, making relationships more profound and lasting.

The chapter also highlights the Hebrew word *H-V-R*, which means "friend" and derives from the root word "obligation." True friendship involves a sense of obligation to one another. By actively engaging in mutual service, individuals foster genuine friendships and build a network of support that enriches their lives.

Appreciate the significance of the relationships you form through your work and daily interactions. Recognize that your connections with coworkers, clients, and business associates are more than just transactional; they are a vital part of a purposeful and fulfilling life.

Focus on being an essential part of your work team. Bring enthusiasm, passion, and dedication to your job.

In your pursuit of a purposeful life, recognize that money is not the end goal but rather evidence that you served others and built meaningful connections. Delight in the joy of serving and helping others, and let this mindset guide your actions, both personally and professionally.

Acknowledgments

Business Secrets from the Bible Workbook

We were feeling the birth pangs of this book during the attack inflicted upon Israel, where we were on October 7. During the months that followed, writing and researching continued after we returned to our home. Even without relatives and friends in Israel whose lives were sent into upheaval, we would have been saddened and concerned. As it was, we were struggling to bring you this book to make your life better while things were happening to people we cared about that were making their lives harder and more painful.

Nonetheless, whenever we spoke to people who had suffered loss, to our surprise, associated with their grief was gratitude. Gratitude that other parts of their lives were uplifting; gratitude that in their small country, they were comforted by so many friends that they didn't even know they had as well as by many people around the world; gratitude that in spite of the pain, their lives were filled with meaning. Gratitude is an indispensable character trait and regardless of what is happening in our lives, a response to the ubiquitous question, "How are you?" should always include gratitude.

Obviously, we feel enormous gratitude at being able to bring this book to fruition, and chiefly that gratitude goes to God. We appreciate the circumstances of our lives that He engineered to make it possible for us to write. We are grateful for our health, and we are grateful for our marriage in which He has played such a role and made it possible for us to live together in complete partnership, not only as marriage partners and parents, but also as professional collaborators. Pulling that off might warrant its own book one day.

We are grateful to our children and grandchildren, who inspire us and encourage us even when they are unaware that they are doing so. We are grateful to

Crystol, Jessica, and Ellen at our headquarters, and we are grateful to Emma and Michaele Angelo, our writing assistants.

We are especially grateful to each member of our team at John Wiley & Sons, our wonderful publisher. All of them, in their own ways, contributed vitally to the birth of this book. Some were midwives, some doctors, some nurses, some anesthesiologists, some were motivators, but all were needed for us to play our role.

It goes without saying that without you and your many fellow readers, we would have been deprived of the main motivation for writing. We are so grateful to you.

Finally, we are grateful to one another, an emotion we both feel many times each day. We pray to be able to continue bringing you more books that make your life fuller and richer through the power of ancient Jewish wisdom. Onward and upward, all of us.

Rabbi Daniel & Susan Lapin

About the Authors

Rabbi Daniel and Susan Lapin

Rabbi Daniel Lapin, noted rabbinic scholar, best-selling author of books like *Thou Shall Prosper, The Holistic You,* and *America's Real War* and host of *The Rabbi Daniel Lapin* podcast, appears live before more than 35,000 people in audiences around the world each year. He is famous for teaching life principles from the Torah, what he calls *Ancient Solutions to Modern Problems,* to people of all backgrounds in entertaining and practical ways.

Newsweek magazine included him in its first list of America's 50 most influential rabbis. With his wife, Susan, he hosted a daily television show, *Ancient Jewish Wisdom.* Through his books, broadcasts, and speeches, he has become one of America's most compelling and persuasive voices of practical biblical principles for both Jews and Christians.

He serves as the president of the American Alliance of Jews and Christians working toward restoring biblical values as the basis of civilization.

Before immigrating to the United States, Rabbi Daniel Lapin studied Torah, physics, economics, and mathematics in yeshivas and schools in South Africa, the United Kingdom, and Israel. He was the founding rabbi of Pacific Jewish Center, a now-legendary Orthodox synagogue in Venice, California.

Rabbi Lapin is a frequent speaker for hundreds of trade groups, political, social, religious, and civic institutions, financial conferences, organizations, and companies. He speaks regularly at synagogues, churches, and universities throughout the country as well as in Europe and Asia. He appears on national radio and television shows.

His articles have appeared in the *Wall Street Journal, Commentary,* and the *Jewish Press*. He and his wife have published seven books, some of which have been translated into Chinese, Croatian, Hungarian, and Korean.

An enthusiastic boater who has sailed his family across the Pacific in their own boat, Lapin raised his family on Mercer Island, Washington. He and his wife recently relocated to the East Coast.

Growing up in the tail winds of second-wave feminism, Susan Lapin contemplated a variety of career options. She never considered being a rabbi's wife and partner as a possible choice, but then she also had no idea that marriage would entail sailing her young family in a small boat across the Pacific Ocean. God had different plans, and for 15 years, she helped lead the legendary synagogue, Pacific Jewish Center of Venice, California, with her husband, its founder, Rabbi Daniel Lapin. During that time, as well as lecturing to women around California on Scripture, personal growth, marriage, parenting, and education, Susan was busy with the Lapins' seven children and homeschooling over the course of 16 years. (Yes, those who wanted to did get into college, where they excelled.) She now lectures to both Jewish and non-Jewish audiences, writes a widely read column, "Susan's Musings," and has cowritten many books, including *Buried Treasure: Secrets for Living from the Lord's Language*, with her husband. She also cohosted the daily *Ancient Jewish Wisdom* TV Show on the TCT television network with her husband. Now living on the East Coast, she finds time to hold an annual summer Grandma Camp for half a dozen little girls who look remarkably like her.

Index